Fighting Words

Words on Writing from 21 of the Heart of Dixie's Best Contemporary Authors

BILL CATON

INTRODUCTION BY BERT HITCHCOCK

Black Belt Press

Montgomery

Black Belt Press
P.O. Box 551
Montgomery, AL 36101

Library of Congress Cataloguing-in-Publication Data

Fighting Words : words on writing from 21 of the heart of
Dixie's best contemporary authors / [edited by] Bill Caton ;
introduction by Bert Hitchcock.
    p. cm.
    ISBN 1-881320-36-7 (hardcover : alk. paper)
       1. American literature—Southern States—History and
criticism—Theory, etc. 2. American literature—20th
century—History and criticism—Theory, etc. 3. American
literature—Southern States—Bio-bibliography. 4. American
literature—20th century—Bio-bibliography. 5. Authors,
American—Southern States—Interviews. 6. Authors,
American—20th century—Interviews. 7. Southern States—
Intellectual life—1865– 8. Southern States—In literature. 9.
Authorship. I. Caton, Bill, 1958–   .
    PS261.F55 1995
    810.9'975—dc20
    [B]   95–23737
                            CIP

Design by Randall Williams
Printed in the United States of America

95 96 97   4 3 2 1

*The Black Belt, defined by its dark, rich soil, stretches across
central Alabama. It was the heart of the cotton belt. It was and
is a place of great beauty, of extreme wealth and grinding
poverty, of pain and joy. Here we take our stand, listening to the
past, looking to the future.*

For Deke

And for my parents
who miss him so

Contents

Preface

THE WRITERS IN THIS BOOK OFFER A LIFE lesson. Their drive, their sincerity, their compassion, their interest in life are compelling. There is much to learn from them. But the first, critical thing is the importance of honesty.

A good question invariably brought a fearless search for a strong, true answer. These are people accustomed to walking into a darkened room of the mind and then turning on the light. They don't peek around corners.

Some of those interviewed write for the commercial market, others write in search of art. While either purpose leads to struggle, these writers share a common trait beyond the willingness to struggle. They are relentless. They battle through fear of rejection, through days of trouble and worry and minutiae. And they remain excited. They remain true to their work, true to their vision, true to the impossible task of telling a story that lives.

It is that battle that inspired the title for this book, *Fighting Words*. These people are picking a fight all right, but not with you or me. They fight with themselves and with the task they have set forth. They fight daily with often unwilling words.

The late Harry Middleton made five thousand dollars a book writing for Simon & Schuster. That would not support his family, so he worked in a shoe repair shop and a grocery store, and in the end he worked collecting garbage for Jefferson County. He wrote late in the night, from midnight to 4 a.m., yet he said he yearned for those hours. When he died from a heart attack at age forty-three, he left his wife and two young children. And he never received a royalty.

Winston Groom, who achieved tremendous fame and fortune with *Forrest Gump*, wondered aloud what he would do if he could no longer sell his work. Before the success spawned by the movie, the fear of losing his publisher—his livelihood—troubled him. Mr. Groom pointed out that every book is a new life with new risks and new challenges to be met. A new book is a chance to write a great life. It is also a chance to lose.

Elizabeth Dewberry and Helen Bell know what a writer's life can do to a family. And Mary Ward Brown knows what a family can do to a woman writer's career. Each has made difficult choices in her time. Mrs. Brown was a mother first, forsaking her art until her son was grown and her husband had passed away. She said the urge to write was overpowering, all-consuming. It was unfair to her family, she said. Ms. Dewberry said she refused to have children to allow herself time to write. Mrs. Bell struggled to raise a family and to write short stories and novels. She still questions her decision.

Robert McCammon, by any estimation, is a tremendously successful writer. He has published twelve novels: *Boy's Life* was critically acclaimed and *Gone South* netted him a fortune. He said he does not have to work again. But he does work, and he struggles with an industry that relies on formulas. Mr. McCammon is reaching for another goal, an artistic goal, but his editors and publishers want more horror genre work. Mr. McCammon's frustration is evident even in casual conversation. Success, in the end, is relative.

Viewpoints change, moods change, answers change. Obviously these people were interviewed in a particular place and time and they have moved on. But I believe that taken as a whole, these conversations offer a detailed portrait of a writer's life. It is as if a single personality emerges from the parts.

That personality emerges because these people are honest. It was a recurring theme in these conversations: A work must be sincere or it will fail. So, the weather changes, the calendar changes, the viewpoint changes. But there is a constant, a point of reference from which we all must begin. I believe these writers provide us with that point of reference. And then they go on to finish the story.

Introduction

By Bert Hitchcock

THERE ARE THREE ROCKS IN THIS SACK, AS some folks might say. Translation: this little introduction has three main observations. They are: that people are generally (and properly) curious about writers; that writers there are aplenty, and many a good one there is, from Alabama; and that Bill Caton provides an old, distinctive, interesting writerly way of getting to meet these interesting individuals.

My first point is perhaps made sufficiently by the fact that you now have this book in hand. (If you must, ask yourself, "Why do I?") *I* think that we non-creative writers think that creative writers are very different, extraordinarily interesting folks—they must be to have done what they have done, to be what they are. These fascinating individuals entrance us with their words, ensnare us in the worlds they create. They entertain us, they worry us, they inform us, they transform us. They do things we can't, things that few can do. They are magicians, prophets, seers—possessors, purveyors, guardians of great mystery. They are of this earth, and not of this earth. How do they do it? Why do they? Who, really, are they? Affected minds, envious and admiring hearts want to know.

Point two: Alabama and literature, a contradiction in terms? Hardly, but there is great educational opportunity in this connection. If, as a friend of mine recently learned from relatives in the

Midwest, there exists serious question about anyone's being able to receive modern medical care in Alabama, what must be the presumption about literature's ministry to the spirit in this state? H. L. Mencken's view of the American South as a cultural desert (the "Sahara of the Bozart" [beaux arts]) helped bring about, Mencken was later jokingly to claim, the literary flowering of the region that began in the late 1920s when such writers as William Faulkner and Thomas Wolfe came to national prominence. This amazing artistic outpouring from the South may not have been absorbed very deeply into the consciousness of the wide American public, though, or having done so, it may have been forgotten or ignored with the Civil Rights Movement of the 1950s and '60s. Or it may just be that Alabama was not seen—like North Carolina, Georgia, and (even) Mississippi—as playing much part in this considerable and continuing phenomenon. The fact is, however, that both in quantity and quality Alabama was an impressive participant in the Southern literary renaissance. And not only that: while the state has claim to some of the best of the Old Southwest humorists (J. J. Hooper, Joseph Glover Baldwin, George Washington Harris) and some of the most popular novelists (Caroline Lee Hentz, Augusta Jane Evans Wilson) of nineteenth-century American literature, at no time have the literary output and the reputations of Alabama writers been greater and more impressive than the present moment of the twentieth century. Many of the most important and impressive persons who make this so, you will meet in the following pages.

Point three, . . . the pages following. Apparently verbatim transcripts of interviews with writers have become a regular part, practically a distinct genre, of professional scholarship and criticism of literature today. These published pieces, as they have evolved, appear in a cool, clipped, symmetrical Question and Answer format—scientifically recorded and objectively transcribed conversations, it is implied. "Conversation" is not the right word here, for the interviewer or questioner, frequently a young academician eager to make an impression and display his or her own knowledge, talks almost as much as the featured writer-interviewee.

What follows in this book is an older type of interview, more journalistic in nature, more the product of a working writer than the new variety is. In its basics, at least, it is the kind of periodical article that Mark Twain helped to establish and to sustain, both as creator and subject, as both reporter and reportee. As subject, Twain was sometimes known to complain. One published newspaper interview with him, he contended, imitated the miracle of the loaves and fishes by reporting infinitely more than what he actually spoke. And sometimes, he observed, what was reported was far different from what he spoke. "They put words in my mouth," he lamented. "I'd rather they put in street sweepings."

What this book's subjects may say in retrospect remains to be said, but they know already that they have been inter-viewed and not just viewed. They know, as will readers of the following pages, that there is at work here an engaged human listener, a personal impression-receiver and sincere interpreter, a fellow struggler-with-words rather than any auto-speaker or purely mechanical transcriber. For the writer of these pieces a process has gone on after the interview, and consequently the same will be true for his readers.

The twenty-one writers featured in the twenty interview accounts that follow—male, female, black, white, at different ages and career stages but all with significant national publication—are, then, joined by another writer, a young journalist. Their presence is made possible through him. To him, through him, but speaking (or seeming to speak) largely for themselves, these individuals talk of their lives and their work, their achievements, their mistakes, their aspirations, and their trials. They speak of desires and of demands, of the compulsions and compensations of a unique profession, an exacting personal commitment. They talk revealingly about life—human life and the writer's life.

"Nobody," Mark Twain claimed, "can be reported even approximately except by a stenographer." And he went on: "Approximations, synopsized speeches, translated poems [and] artificial flowers . . . all have a sort of value but it is small." The modern tape recorder, potentially at least, lessens some of Twain's concerns, but even with such aid today the reporting of any human being can still (as Twain recognizes) only be approximate. Yet we are likely, I think, to find more than just "small value" in the following pages. These are, after all, *writers*. They are people who are *home* folks, geographically for some of us and more generally for all of us because they know, more than most, about where as human persons we *live* and have our being.

Prepare then, to be introduced to, to get to sit down with, a select company. The final feelings of the readers of this book are likely to be akin to those that Mary Ward Brown associates with creative writing itself. The process may not necessarily always be "fun," but it will be satisfying and it will be stimulating—a "deep pleasure." In the following pages natural curiosities get fed and state pride can receive enhancement, but something deeper, wider, and more compelling, I think, will also be addressed.

∽

Dr. Bert Hitchcock teaches in the English Department at Auburn University, where he has served as Chair of Freshman English and Department Head. Having studied also at the University of Melbourne in Australia, he holds degrees from Auburn University, the University of Oregon, and Duke University. In addition to separately published books and essays, he has written articles on American writers for such reference books as the Dictionary of Literary Biography, Reference Guide to American Literature, *and* World Book Encyclopedia.

Money

Courtesy of the Alabama Academy of Distinguished Authors

1

BILL BUTTERWORTH

The difference between a novelist like me and somebody else is I can get myself out of corners better. I look at it as a craft rather than an art. I am not a part of the literary establishment. I don't think I'm anything but a storyteller. I know all the big words, too, but I think they get in the way of the story. We are entertainers, storytellers, and what you're asking somebody to do is give you six or eight hours of their time and it shouldn't have to be work.

What You Need

WHITE BEARD. CIGAR STUBS. BOOKS. GUNS. Hammer-hard sentences. These images of Bill Butterworth linger like blue tobacco smoke.

"The difference between a novelist like me and somebody else is I can get myself out of corners better. I look at it as a craft rather than an art. I am not a part of the literary establishment. I don't think I'm anything but a storyteller. I know all the big words too, but I think they get in the way of the story. We are entertainers, storytellers, and what you're asking somebody to do is give you six or eight hours of their time and it shouldn't have to be work."

Mr. Butterworth writes two novels a year in a house in Fairhope he bought to use as an office. His Mercedes is parked under the carport with the cars of his secretaries. The walls in the stairwell leading up to a sprawling room filled with leather furniture, books and guns are decorated with book covers, movie posters and awards. All the posters show war scenes. Some are from the *MASH* series; others are from his *Corps* series.

"My feeling is that a lot of writers are too much impressed with what we do. The people that read our stuff are as smart as we are. A lot of them [writers] think their stuff is going to be immortal. [This is] not to say I don't think I'm doing a necessary function. I'm just not trying to teach them [the reader] anything.

"I've known a lot of very, very good writers. They are rational human beings. I don't think God laid a hand on me . . . I'm at the end of my life. I'm proud of what I've done. I'm more than I thought I would be. I made a good living for years. I drove Cadillacs for thirty years. In the last ten or twelve years I've made a helluva lot of money."

Is it all about money?

"Publishing is the business of turning ink and paper into money. Anybody who doesn't write for money is a fool . . . It's like selling groceries. What a publisher looks for is somebody who is going to produce three books with a minimum effort. The manuscript should not have holes in it.

"The first time you see your name on a jacket that's a great thrill. After the fiftieth book it's not a thrill. Then getting on the *New York Times* Best Seller list [is a thrill]. I've been on that list nineteen times. What gives me pleasure is getting a letter from a retired Marine who says I did a good job.

"For a while I was writing four and five [books] a year. I had six kids to feed. I wrote six hours a day. That's work, not just being here. I've written every day for a long, long time. Next to the ability to spell, perseverance is what you need. . . . You don't set out to be a writer, you set out to write. Most people have a completely erroneous idea about what being a writer is. You have to start out to write and realize that you're not going to make much money. You have to have the urge to write. Writing is hard work. It's physically demanding. You sit there for long hours. Mental labor is more exhausting than physical labor.

"My friends and I did a little survey of all types of writers that we knew. They had one thing in common: If they are away from the typewriter for more than seventy-two hours they get nervous . . . You can't write and drink. You can't write and take drugs. I drink a little red wine. If I take more than two drinks I can't write the next day.

"I was a soldier for a long time, and the Army kept sending me places. A writer is the sum total of his experience and you never throw anything away. Don't ever worry about not knowing anything, you'll find out what you have to know . . . I have done a lot of research. I read a lot. If I want to write about Rome I can look at a picture in *National Geographic* and I can smell it."

When it all comes together — the hard work, the research, the life experience, the perseverance — the final result is often compelling. Other times it is not. The question, said Mr. Butterworth, is why is some writing good and some writing bad?

"Simple prose is very effective. Every once in a while I write something good and then I write something bad and I don't know how to fix it. If I knew the difference between what it takes to write great fiction and just write good fiction, I'd do it. I don't think I'll stand the test of time. I've never entertained the illusion that I'm a great writer. I'm competent. I try to make it as realistic as I can."

On this spring day Mr. Butterworth was clearly anxious talking about writing instead of doing it. He said more than once that "writers should be read and not heard." He explained, crossing his legs and revealing tall cowboy boots, that he does not give readings because "I'm not an actor, I don't want to hear my own voice. The reader is entitled to know what a writer means. That's what a writer should do." So, how does a writer achieve this difficult goal? Mr. Butterworth touched a lighter to a stub of a cigar and explained.

"You take a two-sentence outline and then you expand on it. I do not reread every day. A writer should make it right the first time. Every sentence affects the book. You shouldn't go on until you've got the problem solved. Slaving over sentences for days is absurd. I don't have the ego that tells me what I'm writing is immortal prose. You can take a look at a sentence and say, 'I can do it better.' By the third time you do it, it should be the best it can be.

"I bought one of the first computers. I've had them for a long time. You used to get one chapter on a disk, now you get a whole book on a disk. Anyone refusing to use a computer because it's beneath his artistic ability, that's bullshit. I did three major revisions on this book [a novel set in Argentina during World War II] and the computer saved months of time. I had a bad structure and I had to fix it and I knew it. I began to shift things around and it worked."

In *Honor Bound*, Mr. Butterworth said he tried to guide the reader through the story by writing his characters' thoughts. To do this, he used dialogue and then occasionally the character would speak his mind in italics. "The editors didn't like the italics. But the only way to tell the story is to tell what the guy is thinking.

"Good editors are rare. The better the editor, the more senior he is. The big shots get to be big shots because they know that what a good editor does is try to improve a writer's book . . . I've got the best editors in the business . . . When a writer starts out, he gets the assholes . . . I'm lucky, I don't fight with them. They are trying to make the best book possible. The writer is emotionally involved and the editor is supposed to be dispassionate. [Thomas] Wolfe couldn't get published today because there is nobody around like Maxwell Perkins to spend that much time. It suggests the genius who doesn't get discovered."

After all the questions about technique, about philosophy, about greatness, what is the real value of living the writer's life?

"It's the best of all possible worlds. I get paid for doing what I like to do. My kids grew up thinking that daddies worked at home, cooked, did everything."

∽

More about Bill Butterworth

Profile:

William Edmund Butterworth III was born Nov. 10, 1929, in Newark, N.J., to William Edmund and Gladys Schnable Butterworth.

Mr. Butterworth was expelled from the Newark Preparatory School and under age at sixteen he joined the United States Army in 1946. He served until 1947. He was trained in counter intelligence and was assigned to the Army of Occupation in Germany. He was relieved from active duty and studied political science for a time at Philip's University, Marburg an der Lahn, Germany. He was recalled during the Korean War and served from 1951 to 1953.

He married Emma Josefa Macalik and they had three children, Patricia Ilga, William Edmund IV, and John Scholefield II. They later divorced.

Mr. Butterworth has traveled extensively and lived for a time in Ozark, Ala. He now lives in Fairhope, Ala.

He has written under the pseudonyms W.E.B. Griffin, Alex Baldwin, Webb Beech, Walker E. Blake, James McM. Douglas, Eden Hughes, Edmund O. Scholefield and Patric J. Williams. Mr. Butterworth has published more than one hundred books. Total sales are estimated at twenty-five million. As of 1994 he had had nineteen consecutive books on the *New York Times* Best Seller List.

Works:

Bill Butterworth (W.E.B. Griffin) has written more than one hundred books since 1961. His work covers a wide range, from juvenile, to nonfiction, to his favorite genre, the war novel. He has written several series of books about soldiers, including co-authoring the twelve-book *MASH* series. He authored the eight-book Brotherhood of War series, the six-book Corps series and the six-book Badge of Honor series.

MASH series (Pocket Books):

MASH Goes to Montreal, 1977; *MASH Goes to Hollywood*, 1976; *MASH Goes to Las Vegas*, 1976; *MASH Goes to London*, 1976; *MASH Goes to Miami*, 1976.

Brotherhood of War series (Jove):

The Majors, 1984; *The Lieutenants*, 1984; *The Captains*, 1983.

Corps series (Jove):

Counterattack, 1990; *Call to Arms*, 1987; *Semper Fi*, 1986.

Badge of Honor series (Jove):

The Victim, 1991; *Special Operations*, 1989; *Men in Blue*, 1988.

Awards:
Honorary Doctor of Literature, Norwich University, 1987.

Excerpt:
He found the light switch, closed his eyes, and turned the lights on. He opened his eyes. In the time it took them to adjust to the sudden glare, he saw two men.

What the hell is he doing next to my bed?

The second man was closer, shielding his eyes. He held a long, curved knife. When he saw Clete, he brought the arm holding the knife up across his chest, so he could slash at Clete when he moved in.

The man next to Clete's bed turned — he had an even larger knife — and assumed a crouching position.

Clete glanced at the closer man, in time to see him start to rush at him.

Did I chamber a round in this thing?

The .45 clicked in his hand, and then again and again. The noise was deafening.

The man rushing him staggered, with a look of surprise on his face. He fell to the ground. The back of his head was a horrible, bloody mess, shattered like a watermelon.

Where the hell did I hit him? In the mouth? I had to; there's no other mark on his face.

The other man was now rushing at him with his knife held high over his shoulders.

The .45 bucked again and again and again and again. The man rushing him started to fall.

Clete pulled the trigger again. The pistol didn't fire. He checked it. The slide was locked in the rear position. He had emptied the magazine.

From *Honor Bound*, in the Badge of Honor series

Joan Wyers Cole

2

CHARLES GHIGNA

"

It's like a game. I can get as creative about marketing as I can about writing. I don't want people to think 'Ghigna's a hustler,' but I want [the work] to get as much attention as it can get. I still beat the bushes. I came up with ideas for marketing and [Walt Disney] jumped on them immediately. Yes, I sit home and think 'What can I do today?' The only reason I do this is because all those years I had to figure a way to get attention for my work. If I do all these things well, the money part takes care of itself . . . my writer friends disdain the marketing aspect. But they know the company better spend money on them or they won't be getting another book published.

"

Child's Play

WITH PRECISION AND ENORMOUS ENERGY Charles Ghigna has built writing poetry into a lucrative full-time job. Mr. Ghigna freed himself from the classroom by researching and expanding into children's literature. And by unabashedly marketing himself.

"It's like a game. I can get as creative about marketing as I can about writing. I don't want people to think 'Ghigna's a hustler,' but I want it [the work] to get as much attention as it can get. I still beat the bushes. I came up with ideas for marketing and they [Walt Disney, publisher of three of Mr. Ghigna's books of children's verse] jumped on them immediately. I talk to an assistant marketing person once a week. Yes, I sit home and think 'What can I do today?'

"The only reason I do this is because all those years I had to figure a way to get attention for my work. If I do all these things well, the money part takes care of itself . . . I know for a fact that my writer friends disdain the marketing aspect. But they know the company better spend money on them or they won't be getting another book published."

Mr. Ghigna lives in a comfortable brick home in a sidewalk-lined suburb of Birmingham. His Jeep has a vanity license plate that reads "PA GOOSE," after his 1994 book of children's poetry. He writes in an attic room with neat filing cabinets, a roll-top desk and a typewriter. In the cabinets are poems and books and ideas. There is unpublished work he wrote and drew for his oldest child more than twenty years ago. Mr. Ghigna never throws anything away and he neatly catalogues poem and book ideas. He was writing brief light verse for the *Birmingham Post-Herald* and was working to get a book of that published so he could sell it into newspaper syndication.

"The syndicates don't want it unless it has a following. If you show them a book, they will assume it has caught someone's eye."

Mr. Ghigna travels, promotes, reads, and lectures. He has fifty paid speaking engagements a year, and if possible, he combines those with book signings for Disney.

"I write in the morning and late at night. I do revisions in the middle of the day. I travel Mondays and Fridays, and in the middle of the week I make phone calls. I don't have an agent. Who's going to do a better job than you for your own work? I get so full of myself sometimes. I get so excited coming back from a reading that I'm on the plane thinking I can write anything . . ."

This energy, this optimism, comes from lifting the burden of teaching from him.

"I'm writing in four genres now. I've had so much to do that something had to give and it wasn't going to be my family . . . I enjoyed teaching and I enjoyed my students. I still stay in touch with some of them. But this is what I've always wanted to do . . . I'm not self-absorbed and cranky anymore."

Mr. Ghigna was having lunch in a Chinese restaurant in Birmingham on a cloudy day. He took a sip of tea, then talked of his two careers.

"The children's poems and the serious poems are at the heart of me. Me falling into writing children's poems was the happiest accident I ever had. Children gave me a new outlet and gave me a fresh look at the serious stuff."

Mr. Ghigna the *marketer* said he follows his son around and "steals" ideas from him. "He has this amazing gift. Every morning he gets up and thinks he can conquer the world. He helps me see the little boy in me. That's when I do my best." Mr. Ghigna the *writer* said: "I don't apologize for any of that [writing children's poems]. I paid my dues for years in the children's magazines. Friends say 'Gosh, you got lucky,' but that's not the case. I wrote for that market for ten years . . . I went to the library and read those magazines. I studied them . . ."

He said getting published was difficult at first, but eventually he began to know some of the editors and discovered "It's a wide-open market. They are looking for good writers."

Mr. Ghigna found success in serious poetry before he entered the world of children. He has published four books of serious poems, one of which was nominated for the Pulitzer Prize.

"There is no question that it is possible to do both [serious and children's poems]. It's just the other way around. Too many times we've limited ourselves, especially serious artists in any field. One of the things that keeps us creative is the joy of the world. The serious artist often takes the world too seriously.

"You get so many literary magazines with so many poems that sound alike. There's a level of skill, but they're not saying anything with passion. I get criticized for being too happy, which is ridiculous. When I get around literary people — and some other poets — I get worn out because they take themselves too seriously. You're writing poems, you're not God.

"There was a time when I was burned out doing the serious ones, but now I'm enjoying it again. Percentage wise, I'm spending 15 or 20 percent of the time playing with serious things, though some days I play with them the whole time. When I work on it now, I work on it with a freshness I didn't have before.

"What I'm doing now is a collection of serious work called *Plastic Soup*. It's going to be done as a book, will be put on-line and will be on CD-ROM. These have a voice that's a little different than I have had.

"With the children's poems, I get real excited real fast and the idea overwhelms me. With the serious ones I don't ever have the whole idea. I have a bit of irony or a scene or a line or two and I want to see where it goes.

"I think I'm good at creating image . . . I usually write six or eight pages of images until it starts clicking and I throw everything away except the little that makes the poem . . . You trust your instincts. You try techniques and strategies. The idea is only the beginning."

"I try to write with a real voice for real people. I try to let the image speak. I don't try to write esoterically. If I've been given credit for anything, it's that people can understand my writing . . . I don't write as an exercise, I use my garbage can faster than I used to . . . It is simple. I'm not taking something simple and trying to make it complex.

"Everybody's writing is autobiographical and anyone who tells you it isn't is lying. Where do you get your ideas? You get them from your life. You've got to start from what you know."

It was beginning to rain when Mr. Ghigna pulled *Tickle Day: New Poems from Father Goose* from his Jeep in the parking lot of the Chinese restaurant. The first copies had just arrived by UPS the previous day. Standing in the fat raindrops, Mr. Ghigna held the book inside the vehicle to protect it from the weather. He flipped to pages, pointing to favorite pictures. He talked fast about the border and art work and how exciting it is to see a book for the first time.

Earlier, in the restaurant, he had said: "This could go away as quickly as it came. If it did, I would still be a writer."

❧

More about Charles Ghigna

Profile:

Charles Vincent Ghigna was born August 25, 1946, to Charles V. Ghigna and Patricia Pelletier Ghigna, in Bayside, N.Y. He was reared in Fort Myers, Fla.

Mr. Ghigna earned both his B.A. and M.A. from Florida Atlantic University in Boca Raton, Fla. He did postgraduate work at Florida State University before leaving to work in the Alabama poets-in-schools program from 1974 to 1976. It was during that time that Mr. Ghigna moved to Birmingham, where he lives today. He taught creative writing at the Alabama School of Fine Arts from 1975 to 1993, when he left to write full time. Mr. Ghigna wrote and published many serious poems in national magazines such as *Harper's* and *The New Yorker*. It was his work in children's literature, however, that allowed him to write full time. Mr. Ghigna contributed children's poems to *Highlights* and other magazines throughout the 1980s before his first children's book, *Good Dogs, Bad Dogs*, was published by Hyperion in 1992.

He is married to Debra Holmes Ghigna and they have a son, Chip. Mr. Ghigna has a daughter, Julie, by a previous marriage.

Works:

Tickle Day: Poems From Father Goose, Disney/Hyperion, 1994.

Speaking in Tongues, Livingston University Press, 1994.

Evening Sun: Haiku, University of Alabama, 1994.

The Day I Spent the Night in the Shelby County Jail, Best of Times, 1994.

Good Cats, Bad Cats, Disney/Hyperion, 1992.

Good Dogs, Bad Dogs, Disney/Hyperion, 1992.

Wings of Fire, Druid Press, 1992.

Sticks I (with X.J. Kennedy), Sticks Press, 1992.

Returning to Earth, Livingston University Press, 1989.

Father Songs, Creekwood Press, 1989.

Circus Poems, Creekwood Press, 1979.

Divers and Other Poems, Creekwood Press, 1978.

Stables: The Story of Christmas, Creekwood Press, 1975.

Plastic Tears, Dorrance Publishing Co., 1973.

Excerpt:

THE WIREGRASSERS

Dry rooted in penny coated clay,
the wiregrassers come
suntan tamed in drawl
through the mire faster.
Machetes high aimed for home,
they carry the clues of day
across their open, flying clothes.
Blade for blade,
steel for grass,
they flog the wire
with a hungry denim run.
Black shinhair stares
boar bristled red out
from rips of hinged tight jeans.
Tobacco spittin' voices
seep coarse through gapped teeth
like hot wax from upside-down brown candles.
An evening shadow sinks itself
in the open field,
closing it for night.
The copper cold dust
from spun home trucks
relaxes into dew
and paints itself across the wiregrass
that sleeps in rust
beneath a hush of moon.

From *Speaking in Tongues*

Jerry Bauer

3

Mark Childress

"

I felt damaged by bad reviews. Every single time I wanted to go find the person who wrote it and kill them.

"

The Things We Do

MARK CHILDRESS WAS DRINKING COFFEE and being cute for the group of ten or so who had left the televised football games and come out into the rain on a muggy September Saturday to hear him read in a cramped antique-shelved Mountain Brook book store.

He sat at a round table with two chairs near the front counter of the store. The conversation ranged from Disney's latest movie to Tolstoy. A bookstore employee corrected Mr. Childress about a title by Dostoyevsky. After about forty-five minutes of hellos, how-are-yous and hugs, Mr. Childress read from *Crazy In Alabama* and received friendly applause. Then he signed his name inside at least fifty books, thanked the owner and left for a sports bar to have a drink with some friends.

"I've been going since 5:15 today in Pensacola."

Mr. Childress was dressed in dingy blue jeans, a much-washed blue shirt covered with white stars and a sports coat with a brightly colored airplane lapel pin. He looked tired and when he smiled shadows deepened beneath his eyes. His slight fingers seemed much more suited for the keyboard than for shaking hands.

"So many writers would kill for an opportunity like this. I'm grateful that they show up and buy the book. Whoever scheduled this on a football Saturday is the dummy."

Football fans screamed at PT's Sports Bar and Mr. Childress drank from a Miller Lite bottle.

"It's more important for the bookstore owners. It lets them put a face with a name and I become a human being. Those people at the store we were just in sold at least two hundred copies of my children's book. They hand-sold them."

A waitress named Chris walked by and pointed to the copy of *Crazy In Alabama* on the table near the ashtray where Mr. Childress' Benson and Hedges menthol smouldered. "I listened to that on tape. It was entertaining, good. I went to the Homewood Library and checked it out," she said. "You didn't buy it?" Mr. Childress chided. Another waitress walked by: "I read this, too. I loved it."

After the first waitress returned for two signatures ("one for me, Chris, and we'll just leave the other one open"), Mr. Childress responded to his apparent fame: "She would never in a million years have known who I was if you hadn't had that book sitting there.

"This is the only business I know where you sit in a room by yourself for two or three years and then you're supposed to come out and be sociable . . . I've tried to write on the road and it's impossible. You go twelve to fourteen hours a day. Inevitably the bookstore owner wants to take you to dinner."

That doesn't fit into a five-day-a-week eight-hour-a-day writing schedule.

"Hard work has the most to do with it [writing well]. You have to think you're going to write a good novel. You have to be willing to sit there and grunt in a chair for four years . . . A writer should spend as much time writing as a plumber does doing his job. I'm not sitting there typing every minute. I just make myself available to it. I work harder for myself than I would for a boss.

"It's like a relief on a day when it really goes well. It's like ramming your head against a steel door and finally someone swings open the steel door and you run through it."

The bar crowd screamed and whooped. Mr. Childress looked at a television screen to watch a Tennessee defensive back chase a Florida receiver.

"I wanted to write novels and have them published. Everything else is gravy. One part of my brain would never believe that I would be doing this for nine years and still be solvent. I just don't think that way [about losing a publisher]. It's enough of a tightrope act to do this. Part of the psychological act you have to do on yourself is that the arc of your career will go OK.

"I only sell one book at a time. I've been offered advances, but that's too much pressure. If you hang it out there and it doesn't work, the money's already spent and you have to pay it back."

Mr. Childress first wrote a novel "because I could. I loved to read novels and I thought that I could do it . . . I had some wonderful mentors along the way . . . John Logue [novelist and retired *Southern Progress* editor] took me to lunch one day and said, 'You've got to write a novel.' . . . It's what I've wanted to do since I was sixteen — write novels. The hard thing would be to put on a necktie and go to the office every day. You write one day at a time. You don't just sit down to write a novel, because if you did you never would."

Why novels and not short stories? "I've tried to write short stories. I don't submit them because they're bad. I need more space to develop my themes.

"I can never read my old work. It seems bad to me. You know, at the time it was the best you could do, but it's still embarrassing to read it."

Rereading unfinished work is crucial, however.

"When I'm rewriting, I read the whole thing. I read aloud. That's the best way to find bumps in sentences. I have a couple of people who read as I'm going along. I'm working on my fifth one now, and I'm beginning to trust myself more. You do get totally sick of it at the end. That's how you know you're finished."

Mr. Childress answered a friend's question, took a sip of beer, then returned to the interview.

"Nobody wants to be quoted in print as saying 'I'm an artist' because it sounds obnoxious. I strive to do art, something beautiful that lasts. Art — the word's gotten loaded. I strive to be an artist. History defines whether it's art. For me to say my work is great art, I can't say that. I think all the time that I want to make art. I do know that if I felt that I had achieved art I would stop . . . I think of myself as a storyteller. Beyond that, who knows? . . . It's up to other people to decide whether it's art."

Childress lit a cigarette. He seemed tired and agitated, but he smiled almost constantly.

"I've gotten some sucko reviews on every one [of his books]. I don't know who [the critics] are. Some Joe says he hates it, maybe because he was in a bad mood that day. I don't write bad reviews anymore. I'm not able to sit down and write a flip review because no matter how bad [the book] is, someone spent two years writing it and someone thought enough of it to publish it. If it's bad, it'll go away anyway. Why write a bad review? I do some book reviewing still. I review for the *Times of London* and the *New York Times*, but I've pretty much cut that out.

"I felt damaged by bad reviews. Every single time I wanted to go find the person who wrote it and kill them.

"I don't think about what a critic's going to say, or how they're going to categorize it [when I'm writing].

"My best book is always the one I just did. The one I'm working on now. I have a soft spot in my heart for *V for Victor* because it sold the least. It's my abused child.

"Each one of my books has done a little better. I do know that what a publisher puts behind it makes all the difference. I've had different publishers every single time. Every editor always seems to have my best interest at heart. I understand that you don't want to get typecast and stuck on a shelf with Southern writers instead of getting out there with *writers*. [Being a Southern writer] is a category. That's for librarians and bookstore owners to decide. If I were from Afghanistan I would write Afghani novels. It's what you know about."

Still, his Southern heritage is evident in his work.

"[Racism] is the central concern of this century in this state, and if you don't address it you're not writing about Alabama."

Southern writers also are easily identifiable by their style, Mr. Childress said. "It's the way we talk. We say, 'Let me tell you what happened.' We tell a story. That's not the way people talk in Yankee Land. We have a real appreciation for someone who can tell a story. But not everybody has patience for the kind of story we will tell."

Mr. Childress lives in Costa Rica, which he calls "the far, deep South. I couldn't afford property in the states. I went there on vacation and loved it. I've been there two years. I built a little house. It's paradise with chickens in the street. It's the Third World. It's real peaceful. I don't know when [I might return to Alabama]. I don't consider myself in exile. Going different places keeps you fresh."

∾

More about Mark Childress

Profile:

Mark Childress was born Sept. 21, 1957, at Monroeville, Ala., to Roy and Mary Helen Gillion Childress.

He graduated from the University of Alabama in 1978 with a B.A. in journalism and English and minored in creative writing. Mr. Childress was a reporter for the *Birmingham News*, was a feature editor for *Southern Living* and was regional editor for the *Atlanta Journal and Constitution*. He quit journalism in 1982 to write his first novel, *A World Made of Fire*.

Mr. Childress lived in San Francisco before moving to Costa Rica.

Works:

Joshua and the Big Bad Blue Crabs, Little Brown & Co., 1995.
Crazy in Alabama, Putnam, 1993.

Joshua and Bigtooth, Little Brown & Co., 1992.
Tender, Ballantine, 1991.
V for Victor, Alfred A. Knopf, 1988.
A World Made of Fire, Alfred A. Knopf, 1984.

Excerpt:

All that remained was her farewell to Chester. Since the moment she found him in the back seat north of Mobile, she'd clung to him as resolutely as he had clung to her. The thought of discarding him had flickered through her mind a hundred times, but every time she passed up a chance to act, it became more impossible.

Once, Lucille had managed to convince herself that D-Con in Chester's coffee was the only way out of her misery. Lately she had come to believe that the presence of his head was somehow connected to her good fortune. She had grown comfortable sharing her adventures with him. They got along much better than at any time when they were married. Until the party in the Hollywood Hills, he had brought her nothing but wonderful luck.

Then in one sordid moment he revealed himself, and her crime. He lit up her foolishness like a stroke of lightning in a dead nighttime landscape. She saw that hanging on to Chester was taking her nowhere but down.

She'd had the courage to kill him, and to get that head off the body, but after that, her nerve had failed. She hadn't been able to take the final step: living without him. She carried him around as a token of her accomplishment, the way a child proudly carries her Crayola drawings and swim-meet ribbons and Girl Scout honor pins.

Lucille knew she had no choice but to lose him in a way that would make sure he never came back.

From *Crazy in Alabama*

Mark Gooch

4

WINSTON GROOM

[October] is speech-making month. I had to give a speech in Amarillo. Out in the audience are Dolly Parton and Fabio, who is some sort of Italian hunk or something. There were twelve hundred people there. It scared me to death. I'm beginning to realize what these guys [famous people] go through. It's the price of doing this business. If people come up, you be gracious about it and do it [sign books and autographs]. Otherwise, you're either a fool or an asshole. I prefer anonymity. I'm a private person, but these are the people who buy your books.

"

A Certain Schizophrenia

MANY SOUTHERN WRITERS SUFFER FROM A dearth of ideas and from the use of boring characters who "start off being dog shit and are going to be dog shit at the end."

So said Winston Groom on a loud, windy day in March, 1992, along the Magnolia River south of Mobile.

"In the forties, fifties and early sixties the South was an extremely exotic place. It was like writing about Tahiti. But in the last thirty years there has been a tremendous economic upheaval. There are few mint julep-drinkers left. I think the New South is boring as hell."

Mr. Groom looked as if his eyes stung, his legs felt achy and his stomach wasn't just right. His long body was awkward in a straight-backed chair under the high ceiling of his home.

"In the seventies Southern writers fell out of favor. As a genre, Southern literature has been out for years and years. I don't consider myself a Southern writer.

"It devolved upon me to review books by Southern writers for the *Los Angeles Times*. These writers, for the most part, are very dour and sour people. The people they write about have Dolly Parton toilet seats. I don't get it. These characters are miserably dreary. The characters are not elevated by the writing. I find these characters are people I don't want to meet. There is no uplifting attitude in these Southern writers.

"[Southern writers] have painted a new and darker picture of the South. Their themes are not of redemption. They are trying to make the South look bad. They have made a career out of showing how stupid Southerners can be."

Mr. Groom's characters have been different from those in traditional Southern fiction. For instance, Forrest Gump, the title character in what Mr. Groom considers his best book, has an IQ of seventy, is six feet, four inches tall, weighs two hundred and forty pounds and can run the one hundred yard dash in 9.5 seconds. He plays football for the Bear, wins the Congressional Medal of Honor in Vietnam, is sent on a space mission to Mars, spends four years in the jungle playing chess against a Yale-educated cannibal, is a professional "rassler," a musician and an actor.

"I wrote [*Forrest Gump*] in four months. When it comes that fast you don't have time to involve yourself in big cerebral carriages. I never knew when I sat down what he was going to do. I found myself laughing at it. It was a delightful book to write. That's what writing's all about. If it ain't fun, fuck it.

"I was editor of the humor magazine at the University [of Alabama]. I've always considered myself a humorist. I like to bring the reader up and down. You have to have people become human in a way where they can laugh at themselves."

Mr. Groom manages to laugh at himself, but that does not mean that he considers his life, the life of a writer, to be easy. There are worries amid the cloud of cigarette smoke.

"You've got to have some torment. You've got to have something inside you that wants to get out. I think to say that a writer is as normal as everybody else is not true. You have to have a certain schizophrenia. The characters live in your head. You don't just put it down and come to dinner. You don't really live in a real world.

"Writing a novel is a lot of work. You have to sustain the will to do it. If you don't bring passion into your work it is evident to the reader and it fails. You've got to do it every day whether you like it or not. If you are writing about a sadistic character and you feel cheerful that day you have to do the work anyway. My mind is going in there. It takes a tremendous amount of concentration. I do it for about two hours. I try to be at the typewriter by eight o'clock or nine o'clock in the morning. It's unproductive to think it will stop. Most of the writers I knew, wrote right up until they died."

Then . . .

"When I was single and living in New York I always thought I could get a job. I had no worries. I'm coming up on fifty and I'm married, I've got to make a living. What if my book flops and I lose my publisher?"

Forrest Gump, filmed by Paramount in the fall of 1993, solved that problem. The movie, starring Tom Hanks, was the highest grossing film of 1994. *Forrest Gump* was re-issued in paperback and more than two million copies were in print late in 1994. Mr. Groom was under contract to write a sequel.

"I haven't been home since the end of July," he said from the Drake Hotel in Chicago in early October of 1994. "I've upgraded my toilet paper some. There's some security here. There's a lot of money flying around. I'm still the same old asshole that I always was."

"[October] is speech-making month. I had to give a speech in Amarillo. Out in the audience are Dolly Parton and Fabio, who is some sort of Italian hunk or something. There were 1,200 people there. It scared me to death. I'm beginning to realize what these guys [famous people] go through. It's the price of doing this business. If people come up, you be gracious about it and do it [sign books and autographs]. Otherwise, you're either a fool or an asshole. I prefer anonymity. I'm a private person, but these are the people who buy your books.

"I'm like a trained bear. In September I did TV and papers. As of November 1 I'm through with speeches. Ideas [for the sequel to *Forrest Gump*] have been coming very, very fast. You have to change your life a little bit. The publishing house says go out and do all of this and the editor says write the book . . . I'm going to start on the sequel in November and be through with it in March. I've already really got it. I've been keeping it in a notebook.

"It's not like torment to do all this. It's work. I've been on this goddamn phone all day long. Everywhere you go, they find you . . . It's rare. It's good. The worst thing is when nobody calls you. You write books and they vanish into some dim fog somewhere. I've got two million books out there now. That's a helluva lot more than all of my other books sold together."

Other encounters with movie-makers have not been as pleasant for Mr. Groom. In a 1992 interview he discussed the making of his 1988 book *As Summers Die* into an HBO movie. *As Summers Die* is about a group of poor Southerners who are forced off their land when oil is found there. Mr. Groom said he felt like some of the characters in the book after his experience with HBO.

"You get these screenwriters who get hold of your book and they don't give a shit. They want to change as much as possible so they can get a screenplay credit. To me, it's like check kiting. But that's something you have to contend with.

"[*As Summers Die*] was made in Georgia. That was a very unpleasant experience. They called me in at the last minute. They were already shooting before I found out anything about it. I took a look at the first two pages of the screenplay and I knew it was trouble. They had the lead character hunting with a retriever. The retriever pointed a pheasant. A pointer points and a retriever retrieves and there ain't a pheasant within a thousand miles of here."

Another bad experience with movies had a better outcome. Mr. Groom got a settlement in April 1992 from ABC after he sued the network for making an unauthorized movie from his 1983 nonfiction book, *Conversations with the Enemy*. The book is the story of Pfc. Robert Garwood, the longest-held Vietnam POW. Garwood was court martialed and convicted of collaborating with the enemy after he returned to the U.S. in 1979. Mr. Groom's book was nominated for the Pulitzer Prize.

"I had a contract with Garwood to write this book and I had the movie rights. Then Garwood started jerking me around. He fell in with some people who were real crooks who sold this to ABC. Then they made the movie. I found this out in July of 1990 at the same time I'm in a movie deal for the book. I invited ABC to a party at the Federal Courthouse. I was pleased with the settlement. ABC has been sitting on the thing for two years. They advertised it but never showed it. I expect they'll be able to show it now, they paid for it.

"That was a very pressing thing on me. It was a weekly deluge of depositions and discovery. If you lose, you lose everything. Most writers simply don't have the wherewithal to deal with this kind of thing."

∾

More about Winston Groom

Profile:

Winston Groom was born March 23, 1943, in Washington, D.C. He was reared in Mobile by his parents, Winston Francis Groom, an attorney, and Ruth Knudsen Groom, an English teacher.

Mr. Groom at the age of ten won the Mobile Press-Register annual prize for a Christmas story. He said winning the prize started him on his writing career. Mr. Groom attended military school in Mobile and then went to the University of Alabama where he majored in English and studied with Hudson Strode. Mr. Groom graduated in 1965 and served as an officer in the United States Army until 1967, including a year in Vietnam. He was discharged from the Army with the rank of captain. He went to work as a reporter at the *Washington Star* where he met Adam Shaw, a reporter for the *Washington Post* and son of Irwin Shaw. Through the Shaws he met James Jones, George Plimpton, Joseph Heller,

Norman Mailer, Truman Capote and others. Mr. Groom quit the newspaper in 1977 to move to the Hamptons in New York and write his first novel, *Better Times Than These*. Mr. Jones read the novel in progress and offered advice, for which Mr. Groom was grateful. Mr. Groom lived in New York City for a time then returned to the Mobile area where he lives today.

He is married to Anne Clinton.

Works:

Gump & Co., Pocket Books, 1995.
Gumpisms, Pocket Books, 1994.
Gone the Sun, Doubleday, 1988.
Forrest Gump, Doubleday, 1986.
Only, Putnam, 1984.
As Summers Die, Simon & Schuster, 1980.
Better Times Than These, Simon & Schuster, 1978.

Awards:

Southern Library Association Best Fiction Award for *As Summers Die*, 1980.

An Excerpt:

Well, we get to the hall where the chess game is to take place an there is bout a thousan people millin aroun an already settin at the table is Honest Ivan, glarin at me like he's Muhammad Ali or somebody.

Honest Ivan is a big ole Russian feller with a high forehead, just like the Frankenstein monster, an long black curly hair such as you might see on a violin player. When I go up and set down, he grunt somethin at me an then another feller say "Let the match begin," an that was it.

Honest Ivan is got the white team an he get to make the first move, startin with somethin call The Ponziani Opening.

I move next, using The Reti Opening, an everthin is goin pretty smooth. Each of us make a couple of more moves, then Honest Ivan try somethin known as The Falkbeer Gambit, movin his knight aroun to see if he can take my rook.

But I see that comin, an set up somethin called The Noah's Ark Trap, an got his knight instead. Honest Ivan ain't lookin none to happy but he seem to take it in stride an employed The Tarrasch Threat to menace my bishop.

I ain't havin none of that, tho, and I thowed up The Queen's Indian Defense an that force him to use The Schevenigen Variation, which lead me to utilize The Benoni Counter.

Honest Ivan appear to be somewhat frustrated, an was twistin his fingers an bitin on his lower lip, an then he done tried a desperation move — The Fried Liver Attack — to which I applied Alekhine's Defense an stopped his ass cold.

It look like for a wile it gonna be a stalemate, but Honest Ivan, he went an applied The Hoffman Maneuver an broke out! I look over at Mister Tribble, an he sort of smile at me, an he move his lips an mouth the word 'Now,' an I knowed what he mean.

You see, they was a couple of tricks Big Sam taught me in the jungle that was not in the book an now was the time to use them— namely, The Cookin Pot Variation of The Coconut Gambit, in which I use my queen as bait an sucker that bastid into riskin his knight to take her.

Unfortunately, it didn't work. Honest Ivan must of seen that comin as he snapped up my queen an now my ass is in trouble! Nex I pull somethin called The Grass Hut Ploy, in which I stick my last rook out on a limb to fool him, but he wadn't fooled. Took my rook an my other bishop too, an was ready to finish me off with The Petroff Check, when I pulled out all the stops an set up The Pygmie Threat.

Now The Pygmie Threat was one of Big Sam's specialties, an he had taught it to me real good. It depends a lot on suprise an usin several other pieces as bait, but if a feller falls victim to the Pygmie Threat, he might as well hang up his jockstrap an go on home. I was hopin an prayin it woud work, cause if it didn't, I ain't got no more bright ideas an I'm just about done for already.

Well, Honest Ivan, he grunt a couple of times an pick up his knight to move it to square eight, which meant that he would be suckered in by The Pygmie Threat an in two more moves I would have him in check an he would be powerless to do anythin about it!

But Honest Ivan must of smelt somethin fishy, cause he moved that piece from square five to square eight an back again nine or ten times, never takin his han off it, which would have meant the move was final.

The crowd was so quiet you coulda heard a pin drop, an I am so nervous an excited I am bout to bust.

From *Forrest Gump*

Frustration

Bill Caton

5

ROBERT MCCAMMON

What I was trying to do was to get them to not be so obvious, so paper-backish. Hardback books are sold to people to keep. You want your work to last and be on a shelf somewhere. It's a strange feeling to be sitting with your editors and talking and they don't get it. They are saying 'Take the easy path.' If you've written three or four horror books then that's what you do, 'Rick, you write horror.' They want to reach the lowest common denominator. I have pleaded and begged them not to use the covers they use and they say, 'Hey, we sell so many books a year.'

Writing Things

A THREE-ARMED MAN IS NOT A MONSTER, A man who walks nude through a small town still has a clear vision of reality, a woman with a disfigured face can soothe pained souls.

And a murderer isn't a bad guy and a flaccid Elvis impersonator can find a good life as himself.

These characters populate the work that Birmingham native Robert R. McCammon, writer of thirteen novels, calls "fictography."

"Nobody gets through life unscarred. Life is tough, made tougher by the scars . . . Parts of me are in that book [*Boy's Life*]. A lot of it's made up. I never grew up in the country. I never really knew my father. The only thing I ever really knew about my father was that he was a drummer in a band. I'm not tortured, but I want to right things."

Mr. McCammon said he created the character Vernon in *Boy's Life* out of a need for justice. Vernon walks the town naked, made crazy by his father and a stupid book publisher. Mr. McCammon was tired of dealing with dull editors.

"The character Vernon is very much me. He was forced to see that you can't be naive and go through life. The first books I had, I had high hopes for and it didn't happen. The publisher will say, 'We messed up, write another one.' Because someone else is in control, it's gone. What about those people who only have one book in them? It's a scary thing that somebody else is in control of your career.

"It's frustrating to be limited to operate under someone else's limitations and tastes. There is this constant disappointment in people [editors] who should know better. I always thought a publisher should encourage you to stretch. They don't have time for that now. They don't have time to build.

"What I was trying to do was to get them to not be so obvious, so paper-backish. Hardback books are sold to people to keep. You want your work to last and be on a shelf somewhere. It's a strange feeling to be sitting with your editors and talking and they don't get it. They are saying 'Take the easy path.' If you've written three or four horror books then that's what you do, 'Rick, you write horror.' They want to reach the lowest common denominator. I have pleaded and begged them not to use the covers they use and they say, 'Hey, we sell so many books a year.'

"What I'm facing now is breaking out of a genre. I could write the greatest book in the world and they would still put it in the horror section. For *They Thirst*, I got letters from people who loved vampire books. With *Boy's Life*, I got letters from everybody. In *Boy's Life* I decided I was going to throw everything in. It just kind of evolved. It flowed together so easily."

Mr. McCammon, eating lunch in Michael's in Birmingham, put down his fork.

"The reality is that you have to get out and sell books just like you sell anything else. I accepted a reading in Greenwich Village, and they had me reading next to the cash register.

"I want to be read. If being literary means you're hard to read, I don't want to do that. I want to be a challenge, but I don't want to be hard to read. [But] you've got to have something in there for the reader to keep coming back to. You build these layers in. You hope people understand about the characters, but if they don't, the story's there. I put depth in on purpose. To me it would be boring as hell to write a plain murder mystery. . . .

"There's a lot going on and I don't understand it. I read a paper by a woman on *Usher's Passing* and how it related to Poe. After I read it, I saw what she meant. I don't think you can plan for all of it. When I finished *Boy's Life* I said, 'Did I do that?' There were parts I didn't remember doing. I didn't understand it all."

Does being a literary writer in the South make one a Southern writer?

"I began not wanting to be a southern writer. You've got this agony and angst about the South. They tried to close it around me a little bit with *Boy's Life* and *Gone South*. The biggest bastards I've ever met are those with the Southern writer mentality."

Mr. McCammon said, however, that he believes it is important for a Southerner to continue to live in his native region. He talked particularly of Birmingham, with its civil rights past.

"It just lets people know you can live here. I love living here. The amazing thing is that if you leave the South and then come back through, then everyone wants to talk to you. You get on all the morning shows. If you stay here, nobody knows you're here."

In a 1992 interview, Mr. McCammon sat in his home in a room filled with board games collected since childhood and hundreds of records and a fireplace and an electronic typewriter and a huge arched window with a view of wobbling, leafy trees. He had just completed *Gone South*, his twelfth novel. He looked tired and frustrated. He questioned whether he had done a good job on *Gone South*. He talked of taking time off from writing. "I've written a novel every year for twelve years."

In 1994 at lunch, he said the time off helped. He was energetic, excited about his thirteenth novel that he was about to send to the publisher. "That extra year helped the plot of the novel germinate. I was just so tired then [immediately after *Gone South*]."

In 1992 Mr. McCammon described himself as two people — Robert McCammon the writer and Rick McCammon, the forty-year-old father of a toddler.

He said then that he did not like dealing with fan mail and

giving interviews. He said those things invaded his privacy. After a pause, he said that he was getting better at accepting the outside contact. "I'm not as disconnected from the author as I once was. I wanted some distance when I first started out. I wanted to put distance between Rick, who was the kid, and Robert, who is the person who is doing this book. Maybe I didn't think very much of myself as a kid.

"The need for acceptance stays with you even after twelve novels. When I was in high school I was reading a story and the room was silent; I had their attention. I still think that's neat, to have people share something with you."

But sharing only goes so far. Mr. McCammon refuses to get involved in Hollywood even though he has sold the movie rights to *Boy's Life* and *Gone South*.

"They pay you for things and they sit on a shelf for years. They pay for things so other people won't get them. No writer's ever gone to Hollywood and not been changed in some way or destroyed. If you wanted to be involved you'd have to go there. I would not dream of being a screenwriter. That would be one of the inner circles of hell. They take away your freedom. My prime enjoyment in life is being in control of what I do. I've already done a movie, a movie you can see in your mind."

∾

More about Robert McCammon

Profile:

Robert R. (Rick) McCammon was born July 17, 1952, in Birmingham, Ala., to Jack and Barbara Bundy McCammon. Mr. McCammon's father was a drummer in a band and left the family early in the writer's life.

Mr. McCammon earned a B.A. from the University of Alabama in 1974. He was editor of the school newspaper, the *Crimson White*. During 1974-75 he worked in advertising at Loveman's

Department Store. In 1976 he worked at Dalton Booksellers. He was a copy editor at the *Birmingham Post-Herald* from 1976 to 1978, when he published his first novel, *Baal*. Mr. McCammon worked during off hours from the newspaper to begin his career as a novelist. Early in his career Mr. McCammon was known primarily as a horror writer. But he was working to break out of that mold with *Boy's Life* and *Gone South*.

Mr. McCammon lives and works in his native Birmingham. He and his wife Sally have one child, Skye.

Works:

Gone South, Pocket, 1992.
Boy's Life, Pocket, 1991.
Mine, Pocket, 1990.
Blue World, Pocket, 1990.
The Wolf's Hour, Pocket, 1989.
Stinger, Pocket, 1988.
Swan Song, Pocket, 1987.
Usher's Passing, Holt, 1984.
Mystery Walk, Holt, 1983.
They Thirst, Avon, 1981.
The Night Boat, Avon, 1980.
The Hungry, Avon, 1980.
Diana's Daughters, Avon, 1979.
Bethany's Sin, Avon, 1979.
Baal, Avon, 1978.

Excerpt:

This was early summer in Zephyr: an awakening to hazy morning heat, the sun gradually burning the haze off and the air getting so humid your shirt stuck to your skin by the time you'd walked to the mailbox and back. At noon the world seemed to pause on its axis, and not a bird dared to wing through the steaming blue. As afternoon rambled on, a few clouds rimmed with purple might build up from the northwest. You could sit on the porch, a glass of lemonade at your side and the radio turned to a baseball game, and watch the clouds slowly roll toward you. After a while you might hear distant thunder, and a zigzag of lightning would make the radio crackle. It might shower for thirty minutes or so, but most times the clouds just marched past with a rumble and grunt and not a drop of rain. As evening cooled the earth, the cicadas droned in their hundreds from the woods and lightning bugs rose from the grass. They got up in the trees and blinked, and they lit up the branches like Christmas decorations here on the edge of July. The stars came out, and some phase of the moon. If I played my cards right, I could talk my folks into letting me stay up late, like until eleven or so, and I would sit in the front yard watching the lights of Zephyr go out. When enough lights were extinguished, the stars became much brighter. You could look up into the heart of the universe and see the swirls of glowing stars. A soft breeze blew, bringing with it the sweet perfume of the earth, and the trees rustled quietly in its passage. It was very hard, at times like this, not to think that the world was as well-ordered and precise as the Cartwright ranch on "Bonanza," or that in every house lived a "My Three Sons" family. I wished it were so, but I had seen pictures of a spreading dark, a burning man, and a bomb-wrecked church, and was beginning to know the truth.

From *Boy's Life*

Gloria Jones

6

RODNEY JONES

"

You can never judge the merits of what you do. It's basically the immersion. The value of the piece you work on is very different from the value other people put on it . . . A lot of what you do depends on your love of the art. The art that's valuable to me seems to be self-transcending. I would hope that art would come to a place where it doesn't seem like art . . . Art is a dangerous concept to me. I'd rather think of a writer like a plumber or a craftsman . . . If I get to a point where I really think I've done something that I think I have to come up to again, that could be dangerous.

"

It's the Immersion

RODNEY JONES IS COMFORTABLE STANDING under a descending softball in the green outfield of an Illinois baseball diamond. During the game he jokes with the seriousness of a twelve-year-old who's playing to win. He knows who can hit the ball out and who can run. And he knows that for this time on a Saturday afternoon he is not a poet. He can dress in shorts, wear his cleats and his gorky sports glasses, and look more like a metamorphosing teenager than a man in the rare position of feeling beauty and art as steam, as pressure seeking a valve.

"In my first book there was a great joy in writing poems. In the last book I started out with a technical mistake. Then in the middle of it a friend died and that plunged me down. Then I had a child and that plunged me up. My life was a struggle and the book was a struggle.

"I think there is an emotional bone that comes up in people. I tend to be more subject to depression. I find a lot more facility when I'm feeling good.

"*Apocalyptic Narrative* was a five-year poem. I'm not sure that it was worth it. That was a very difficult poem to write because I was not sure what I was after. You can write some in five hours that are great. I had a sense that there were important issues in the poem that came out of my childhood living with nuclear weapons. It was like this huge intellectual carbuncle . . . .

"If you take on a really big topic and write your heart out on it with tremendous ambition, then it comes out and you don't think it's one of the great poems of the century, then it's not satisfying . . . Some days you'll think, 'God, I did good that time,' and some days you'll think, 'Well, that's fodder.'

"You can never judge the merits of what you do. It's basically the immersion. The value of the piece you work on is very different from the value other people put on it . . . A lot of what you do depends on your love of the art. The art that's valuable to me seems to be self-transcending. I would hope that art would come to a place where it doesn't seem like art . . . Art is a dangerous concept to me. I'd rather think of a writer like a plumber or a craftsman. . . . If I get to a point where I really think I've done something that I think I have to come up to again, that could be dangerous.

"I went to this show where this guy hung himself from his butt by hooks. These women were there and they were talking about how fabulous it was and how it was art. Self-desecration is bullshit. The guy is fucking nuts and you're saying that's art? The word art takes on a great freedom of expression and that's good, but I get nothing out of a guy who hangs himself up by his butt.

"[Artists] are trying to create something beautiful and original that trues to life. . . . Many artists of the twentieth century try to dismiss the idea of beauty and I can't do that. Literature is entangled in things like beauty of expression. The poems I like best stun me on the art side and yet I can believe them. . . . Poetry, the idea of the right words in the right order, is pretty goddamn awesome.

"Last year I was in Mexico and I was finishing *Apocalyptic Narrative*. It was at a stage where there was nothing but work on lines and sentences and I started on a novel. I got three hundred pages and the best I could tell, I was one-third of the way through. One of the reasons I quit was it was clear I needed to do some thinking. It was getting out of hand. There was just one digression after another. It was great fun, perhaps more fun than writing a poem.

"In the novel I was interested in how much did I give up in the ideal of language. I wouldn't do it with the idea it's less art than poetry. . . .

"I'm not convinced there is such a huge distinction between genres. Good writers are valuable no matter what they're writing."

Mr. Jones teaches one semester a year, so he has a lot of time to spend writing in the low-ceilinged, cramped room behind his house in Carbondale, Ill. He writes among newspaper clippings and a jumble of books. His curly hair and thick mustache and full ashtray seem to crowd the room.

When he is writing well, Mr. Jones writes "two shifts a day, 8 a.m. to noon, and I write again from ten — after my wife and children are in bed — until one. Last spring I got into a spell and suddenly good stuff was coming easy. I tend to get run down in those periods. The wires start shorting out and then I step away from it. I write every day for eight months a year, but not twelve.

"I don't value writers for the number of books. The point seems to be to do it right. . . . It's interesting to think a hack writer might have been as good as Thomas Wolfe if he approached it with his whole being.

"It's probably a habit. People like Faulkner, I don't think they ever knew what they were doing. Innocence is involved in it. There can be a writer who is Phi Betta Kappa who approaches it with no innocence. They have a grip on everything that's happening, but it's shy of the desperation. . . . That's a very hard thing to do, to articulate that miasmic emotion at the center. That's a big deal.

"Writers are influenced by other people, but it is equally important to be able to milk one's own experience to see the possibilities on the planet as opposed to just the experience on the page. You have to see that something might arise from experience that's energizing. [Writers] have to find access to the vision of the world that they found individually. There has to be a way from the style to that.

"It's important not to feel too much like the little dog if you're going to write. Writing is an independent and lonely pursuit. Most writers try to dodge those questions [of influence]. . . . If you fall under somebody's shadow you're in trouble. . . .

"At times I get so moved by another writer; there are lines in poems that should have been theirs. I have one poem, "Laundromat at the Bay Station" in *The Unborn* that I wish I could give to C.K. Williams. It's good, but it's not mine.

"There are things that happen when a great work happens that are beyond what's derivative. When you read it, it has to be absorbed somewhere down deep. Anybody would fail anybody else's test. If it's not owned solely by that person [the writer], then it's going to fail. Ownership is when there is primary authority for the material. I'm not sure how much of that can be dealt with consciously.

"You have to find a balance between writing and reading. Writers certainly don't know the most about literature.

"Writers being attached to academics like I am seems to be something that could be detrimental. It seems important for writers to have experience that is a little more out there than in an educational environment. Life around colleges is a little easy and a little churchy. . . . If I were rich I'd teach when I wanted to. I suspect that I would like to teach — some."

Mr. Jones, who retains a Southern accent even though he lives among Illini, says his teaching and writing styles are directly attributable to his Southern upbringing.

"It seems like whenever I'm in New York or St. Louis I'm sitting next to two women who are so earnest in their conversation. They are talking about other people, trying to solve problems. If you are in the South, people are telling stories. It's a natural thing, talking in parables.

"A lot of the good poets who are Southern are defined by liberal politics. . . . I lived so far out in the country the bootlegger was a black man. I knew his kids and we played together. I got disturbed that they were having to get up at 5 a.m. to catch a bus to go to the one black school in the county.

"In junior high, kids started calling me Martin Luther because I was militant about racism. I thought I was right and I saw that heroic nature of the struggle. That heroic attitude that I had grew out of watching Superman and stuff."

Too much of a good thing?

"There's a great value to having that ear, but if you can't put it [dialect] down without causing someone to suffer, then it's no good. I'd like to use speech patterns of blacks or male homosexuals. They don't own that.

"If you're a Southerner, it's a common perception that you're stupid. It's a prejudice against white males from the South. It's a prejudice like that against the Germans after World War II. There's a lot of feeling of inferiority among Alabamians."

Later, in a sports bar . . .

"I don't like to be a poet in the town where I live. I like to live a life separate from being a poet. Most people don't have a notion about it. If people think you're a freak it's very hard to have a normal relationship.

"After you win an award, everyone is congratulating you. It's like going down this corridor of congratulations. After a while, it gets like a loved one has died."

Mr. Jones has been congratulated many times. And in a sense, success was immediate. Although he began writing poems when he was in high school, he was not published until much later, in college. In college he would give poems to friends who were editing literary magazines. Then, in 1972 he got married and needed to be paid for his work. He sent some poems to *The Atlantic Monthly*. *The Atlantic* bought three of his poems immediately and the poetry editor, Peter Davidson, now his editor at Houghton Mifflin, offered to look at other poems for a possible book.

"That's a strange story, getting picked out of the stack like that. It was weird to start with when I started getting poems in national magazines. I was concerned about whether I would remain motivated. I haven't yet written anything that I can take to my home church and read as great art."

One reason he can't go to his church and read a poem as great art is there are "twelve people in the universe who are not poets who read poetry . . . I'm trying to write poems that are easier to read . . . It seems to me to be important to write things that are for people to read and that make sense. I think I could create a better book that more people would like to read. Someone writing poetry is not in it to make money, but everyone wants to have their books read. I'd like to write a book that fifty thousand or one hundred thousand people would buy."

Apocalyptic Narrative sold about four thousand copies. How satisfying is that?

"There were several poems in the book that I really liked. When I finished this book it seemed to me there was a character in the book that I liked, but I didn't like all the poems. These books you write get beyond you and eventually they seem to have been written by other people."

∾

More about Rodney Jones

Profile:

Rodney Jones was born Feb. 11, 1950, in Hartselle, Ala., to E.L. and Wilda Owen Jones. His father was a farmer and factory worker and his mother a housewife.

Mr. Jones earned his B.A. from the University of Alabama in 1971 and his M.F.A. from the University of North Carolina at Greensboro in 1973. He was writer-in-residence at Virginia Intermont College in Bristol, Va., from 1978 to 1984. He left that job to become assistant professor of English at Southern Illinois University at Carbondale, where he remains. Mr. Jones wrote poetry during his entire college career but never sought serious publication until he married in 1972. *The Atlantic Monthly* bought three poems and offered to consider collecting his other work for a book. He has published five collections of poems since then.

Mr. Jones is married to Gloria Nixon de Zepeda, an artist. They have two children, Samuel and Alexis.

Works:

Going Ahead, Looking Back, Southbound Books, 1977.
The Story They Told Us of Light, Univ. of Alabama Press, 1980.
The Unborn, Atlantic Monthly Press, 1985.
Transparent Gestures, Houghton Mifflin, 1989.
Apocalyptic Narrative and other poems, Houghton Mifflin, 1993.

Awards:

Lavan Younger Poets Award from Academy of American Poets, 1986; National Endowment for the Arts fellow; Guggenheim fellow; Younger Writers Award from General Electric Foundation, 1986; Jean Stein Prize from American Academy and Institute of Arts and Letters, 1989; National Book Critics Circle Award, 1989.

Excerpt:

FANTASIA OF THE BRIDE

I glimpsed you just as I was dying, cluster of grapes
Dipping toward the clear river, startled white birds,
Wisest and wildest and loveliest who lay with me
All those years while flesh opened like a door
And the old poignant steam of creation rose
Above the calibrated hours of numbing appointments
As when the odors of coffee and croissants briefly
Ascend the carnal spices of the delicatessen,
And the throat hurts for the beauty of one night,

Which will not last; even as the feeling begins
It is gone into the morning's etherizing rind.
A blind music holds the brain down to its joy,
The hand plunging or the cheek glowing with blood,
Consumption, sexual and mortal, in which we flare,
Blue as fuses at the silent core of the trance,
And the world of scorned treasures burns back:
A boot, a shredded Goodyear tire, the Atlantic
Behind you that same evening a dead porpoise
And Russian detergent bottle washed ashore.
You were wearing your blue jeans and white shirt.
Small bones curdled of starlight, salt privacy
Of elbows and knees, secret estuary of skin,
Your hair was combed back from your face
And hung in a straight ponytail down your back.
It was the first year, I think, that you thought
Not to put red on the lips, black around the eyes.
Hands with short nails, voice of plain speech,
Bringing on the final exorcisms of courtship,
I noticed you among the actual stars — illicit,
Undeniable, intolerable, but grounding all this
Ten-year unwarrantied life. I have said next
To nothing, plumber of dark gray drains,
Resuscitator of dead stoves. It was never
As though breasts would rebuild Dresden
Or thighs resurrect the ride up San Juan Hill.
It was never as though you thought of me
As a train weapon or car. To speak of love
Is to speak of knowing, but stand oblivion
On its end; let me be that ocean, dark
And unlettered and arriving only at itself,
Though I keep you in mind, the flesh bond
And public secret, our dumb beauty in the best hours.

From *Apocalyptic Narrative*

Mark Gooch

7

MADISON JONES

"

It was not a deliberate choice. I would love for one of my books to be popular. I can't write thinking that this is the way to do it to please a lot of people. I write about subjects that are interesting to me. . . . It's legitimate [to write for a mass audience]. I probably would if I could. What engages the imagination seriously is what makes you do it well. I assume that a writer for a large audience is turned on by what he's writing about. My subjects have been almost invariably serious. I make a connection between the writing of fiction and serious ideas. I think of writing as something illuminating and durable. Sometimes good books do have a big sale.

"

The Very Best Effort

MADISON JONES SPOKE IN SOFT TONES ON the telephone from his house after supper on an early October evening in 1994: "I don't write any more books. I think the bird has flown."

Jones, a creative writing teacher at Auburn University for thirty-one years, wrote ten novels, and eight had been published.

"I still think about it some. I'm almost seventy years old. I wish I had published more. I published eight and I guess I'll publish this ninth one . . . I think I've said about what I had to say. Sometimes I think that. Also, add the fact that I feel that I'm out of it in time. I write in a certain way and style, and I have a certain kind of subject matter that was much more the thing twenty or thirty years ago. I'm old-fashioned."

"My production — I wish it had been greater. I write slowly. My books represent my very best efforts."

Mr. Jones lives in a ranch-style house in the woods off a dirt road outside of Auburn. There are many busts in the large living room, some with painfully distorted faces. Mr. Jones' own face is an interesting blend — white beard, flushed skin, jagged yellow smile, tiny, round, penetrating eyes.

"I taught thirty-three years. [I enjoyed it] part of the time. Sometimes I did. I got tired of it finally. I felt that if I had to read one more creative writing story I'd blow my head off. Maybe I would have done more if I hadn't taught. At first, earlier in my career, I did a lot of heavy teaching. It was pretty tough. After I began to get a reputation it improved my circumstances.

"I've got a book running around. It's not easy to get on in the East now. There is a money crisis in all the houses. They won't take any chances. There used to be a mid list — books they knew were good but probably weren't going to make much money — and that is just gone. Writers everywhere are scrambling to find publishers."

In a 1992 interview, when Mr. Jones was in the middle of writing his tenth novel, he said: "I have always thought literature was serious business. You try to say something worth hearing. Try to lead the reader into a kind of wisdom . . . I was educated that way when I was in college. I was a serious literary man and read serious novels by [Joseph] Conrad and [William] Faulkner. Popular fiction just wasn't something in my kin."

Two years later: "It was not a deliberate choice. I would love for one of my books to be popular. I can't write thinking that this is the way to do it to please a lot of people. I write about subjects that are interesting to me. . . . It's legitimate [to write for a mass audience]. I probably would if I could. What engages the imagination seriously is what makes you do it well. I assume that a writer for a large audience is turned on by what he's writing about. My subjects have been almost invariably serious. I make a connection between the writing of fiction and serious ideas. I think of writing as something illuminating and durable. Sometimes good books do have a big sale."

Can a work be illuminating and durable if the writer is categorized as regional?

"I know why people take the point of view [that they don't want to be categorized as a Southern writer]. They think that makes them limited to folk writing. That's perfectly ridiculous. Regional writers are some of the best in the world. Thomas Hardy, Faulkner. Robert Penn Warren's novels are nearly all about the South. The subjects of fiction exist in small places as well as great ones. Being a regional writer is not a limitation . . . You write about what you know about and if you don't know about it, you won't write a very good book. Regionalism is the true strength of a nation and the true strength of art. It's provinicial to deny you're a regional writer."

More on the South and writing . . .

"Southern literature has an awful lot of tragedy in it. It comes from the Civil War, a sense of dislocation. Thinking about man's rather unsatisfactory plight. People say the South has a lot of things on its conscience, but not many Southerners would trade locales to Michigan or Connecticut.

"When I was young, the Civil War still had a good deal of freshness. My grandfather knew people who were in it. It enriched life. It was sort of like you had a personal history that went back one hundred years. A lot of Southerners feel guilty even though they have nothing to feel guilty about."

Asked if Alabama and, in particular Birmingham, have been marked with an indelible historical stamp because of events during the civil rights struggle of the 1950s and 1960s, Jones replied: "Bullshit. I'm very proud. I'm not proud of everything everybody did. But there were a lot of good people on both sides. Suppose in the sixties I had taken a segregationist sign and walked through Harlem. They would have killed me and dismembered me. They refer to slavery like it was some unknown, evil institution cooked up by the American South. Until the eighteenth century it was worldwide. All of this has gotten so exaggerated [by writers]. Are you responsible for something some angry redneck does? Nothing vexes me more than that guilt crap."

He said Southern writers often choose the "guilty South" point of view because "that's where the power lies [in the North]. They're the people to please, not your home folks. You get singled out for being good in the middle of such evil. That kind of toadying helps you get published."

In the 1992 interview in his home, he said:

"In the process of trying to eliminate verbiage, you crowd it into speaking to you. You work on how to make every word speak. There is a connotative quality of words that suggest more than they denote."

❧

"One thing for me is I know more about words than I used to."

❧

"My pace has been a page a day. I go over each sentence as I write. I always put a lot of emphasis on rhythm. I measure syllables by speaking them to get a certain kind of beat. Three hundred to 350 words is my usual day. That would occupy several hours."

❧

"I've read nearly everything to my wife. I read daily. It helps get perspective. I usually read the previous day's work."

❧

"I don't like to do it [write] the same way I like to eat a good piece of pie or play a game."

❧

"You've got to have an idea that makes a story. I don't start off with a perfected idea. I start off with a situation in mind. I try to think of some characters in it. I never know how it's going to end, or events that occur in the middle of the book. I discover as I go along what seems to be the next thing to do."

❧

More about Madison Jones

Profile:

Madison Percy Jones, Jr., was born March 21, 1925, in Nashville, Tenn., to Madison Percy and Mary Temple Webber Jones.

Mr. Jones received his A.B. from Vanderbilt University in 1949. He earned his A.M. from the University of Florida in 1951. Mr. Jones was a horse trainer during the 1940s. He was an instructor of English at Miami University in Oxford, Ohio from 1952 to 1954 and the University of Tennessee from 1955 to 1956. He was an assistant professor and later creative writing teacher at Auburn University from 1956 until his retirement in 1987. Mr. Jones was in the U.S. Army Corps of Military Police from 1944-45. He also served in Korea. Mr. Jones wrote his first novel long-hand while lying on a cot during the day on a farm in Tennessee.

He is married to Shailah McEvilley and they have five children, Carroll, Madison III, Ellen, Michael and Andrew. The Joneses live just outside Auburn.

Works:

Season of the Strangler, Doubleday, 1982.

Passage Through Gehenna, Louisiana State University Press, 1978.

A Cry of Absence, Crown, 1971.

An Exile, Viking, 1967, published as *I Walk the Line*, Popular Library, 1970.

A Buried Land, Viking, 1963.

Forest of the Night, Harcourt, 1960.

History of the Tennessee State Dental Association (nonfiction), Tennessee State Dental Association, 1958.

The Innocent, Harcourt, 1957.

Awards:

Sewanee Review fellow in 1954; the Alabama Library Association Award in 1967; Rockefeller Foundation fellow in 1968; Guggenheim fellow in 1973.

Excerpt:

She saw, with a quickening of panic, that she must get inside to do it, but now she did not hesitate. There was space between his rump and the edge of the seat, and here she perched herself, touching against him, while her foot pressed the pedal and her hand slipped the lever into neutral. And then the key. Her fingers trembled on it. Hesitating, she imagined a stroke like a gun's blast. And it would wake him. He would sit up, alarmed, and she would invite him into the house, to his bed. She turned the key.

A grating noise and then the engine resounded. It was not the shock she had expected, for she saw that he had not moved. She stared at the paleness that marked his head, propped against the door, and listened how the sound of the motor had achieved a kind of subdued and rhythmic beat. She would turn it off. The impulse moved her hand back to the switch, but she checked it there.

"Mama."

It was barely audible. She had stiffened, holding her breath. Later:

"Where we going?" he mumbled, ever so faintly.

She thought of answers, but all were mocking answers. To Fountain Inn, she thought. To see them pick the cotton. Minutes later she was still silent, frozen, hearing the hollow throb of the motor. Were those not fumes she smelled — already fumes — entering his nostrils on the long breaths he drew. But this was his body still warm against her side, his rump whose shape in infancy seemed even now impressed upon her hand. It was the hand that rested on the switch. With a sudden twist she turned the key. The motor coughed and died, and she gave a lunge that carried her clear out of the car and left her hanging upon the open door in a kind of swoon whose soundlessness was that of a void into which she had fallen.

From *A Cry of Absence*

Mark Gooch

8

ELISE SANGUINETTI

"

I don't think there's such a thing as outliving talent. I've known novelists who go on and on putting out stuff and it's terrible. It's not a crime. I couldn't stop writing. It wouldn't be right, I wouldn't be breathing.

"

Getting Better

ELISE SANGUINETTI WAS ON A RIGID SCHEDule in October 1994. She was midway through a novel about women in the South from the Roaring Twenties to the present. As she worked on the novel, she also worked to vanquish a nagging doubt.

"Now I've written a book and put it aside. I knew it didn't work and I sent it to my agent who said it wouldn't sell. That's terrible. I spent two-and-a-half years writing a book and had to put it aside. It wasn't commercial enough. It was called *Mothers and Daughters* and was almost like *McBee's Station*, the old going away and the new coming up. The dumb thing is that my agent told me halfway through it that it wasn't working. And I knew it wasn't working. Putting aside the novel was a real blow.

"I wrote the novel and it just sits out there staring at me. It was about old age, and nobody in the world was interested in old age. Once you've done that [written a novel that won't sell], you lose all interest [in that novel] and you can't go back to it."

A few minutes later . . .

"Your writing deepens [as you age]. You have more depth and you've experienced more. You've read more and said more. I hope this [novel in progress] is going to be the best one I've ever written. My agent thinks so. I think the one you're working on is the best. I never have read them again. It's like eating Kleenex. It's too boring. There is no surprise anywhere.

"I don't think there's such a thing as outliving talent. I've known novelists who go on and on putting out stuff and it's terrible. It's not a crime. I couldn't stop writing. It wouldn't be right, I wouldn't be breathing.

"[Writing] is enormous. It's overwhelming. I dread it. I hate it. I sharpen pencils, look at flowers outside. I'm glad I've done it afterwards. It's like going to church. Nobody wants to go to church, but afterwards they're so glad they went.

"You've got to write every day, just like you're going to work. You write from nine until noon and then you get through the afternoon and you start again. It's hideous. I write on Saturdays, but I don't write on Sundays. I'm very unproductive. I'm a very slow writer.

"Some days it goes better than others. I call three or four pages a good day and some days, in transitions, one page is the limit . . . It's going to take forever with this one, trying to make it real, come to life again. Wars and depressions and all that stuff. [Writing] is a hard time. I don't use an outline. I don't know what's going to happen next. These people [characters] grow along with me. Fitzgerald wrote by carefully planned outlines. I can't do that.

"I write on my college typewriter. It's a Royal portable. It's been with me through so much and I can't give it up. It's like this person there."

Mrs. Sanguinetti parts her white hair on the side and she moves and talks with the energy of a child. She does not consider herself a professional writer, yet she has the discipline of a monk. She said she has written hundreds of short stories. It was a short story — her first one accepted — in *Mademoiselle* that led to her first novel, *The Last of the Whitfields*.

"I'm not very good at short stories, but I still write them. I started out writing short stories. I thought that was the thing to do. I kept doing it. I would get letters of encouragement [from magazine editors]. Just keep sending them out 'till you get it. It takes you a week to get over it [a rejection]. You really are writing in the face of tremendous odds. I just kept doing it. I did it for two years, three years and one hit."

What causes one to choose a profession that offers such little hope of success?

"I have no idea except some gene that went astray. My father was a newspaper man, and I remember hearing the typewriter at night. What made me go inside a room and shut the door and write 'He said, she said'? I don't know. My characters are still real to me. They're still in my head. It gets confusing. Writers are all crazy. Writing is all about making something out of nothing. It's not artistic. Artistic is selfish, it's putting you above other people. I don't like the words artist and writing together.

"I think [writing for newspapers] helps because of the experience you get. But you shouldn't work there long. I had a hard time getting that journalism style out of my system. I do think it's great because of the different people you see and the things you know. You learn things about people. If you are the religion editor, then say good-bye. Hard news and features can help. But it's awfully hard on your style."

She wrote four novels from 1961 to 1971, but did not write a novel during the 1980s.

"I got tired of writing novels. Just got sick of it and everything that goes with it — 'Will you speak to us about this,' 'Will you read that.' I just wanted to be left alone.

"I don't go to those things. You're asked to speak and you go to these meetings about Southern literature. You don't ever hear of a meeting about the Midwestern novel, the Western novel and the Eastern novel. I don't know why we do this in the South. I'm sick of it."

"I never really did it [go to readings and publicity events]. My publisher was furious. It probably does hurt sales. I feel sorry for anybody who's doing it — getting up in these strange cities and finding TV and radio stations and they haven't read the book. I think it's stupid. They [the publishers] do that instead of advertising for you. In other words, they do nothing.

"I never thought I'd get rich from writing. I wouldn't mind it, though. I'm not the type of writer that appeals to masses like that. Good writing is out the window. Quality of writing doesn't matter in selling. It's better if you don't have good writing. All these murder things, they're bad writing. People don't care about good writing. If [the characters] get married in the end, it's a good book."

How does one sell a book with no happy ending?

"An agent is essential unless you just write this great thing. You have to have one, and a good one. An agent will read it and tell you whether it will go or not. They'll argue for a better price."

Art often imitates life, but Mrs. Sanguinetti had a somewhat different experience. She had just published *The Last of the Whitfields*, and her editor came to Anniston to visit her. While in Alabama he went to Birmingham and other cities and then wrote a story about the racist South for *Mademoiselle*, much the same as a character in the book had done.

"I invited them to the house and they came to Birmingham and wrote this terrible thing about Birmingham. This was after my book was out. It was terrible. We were all just evil people. I just wanted to hide.

"Why are people so absolutely consumed with race? It's part of our experience. Northerners think we're horrible. I think it's intellectually dishonest [for Southern writers to exploit race for profit]. You have to have honesty and integrity. I don't think it [a one-sided work] would be of any value. Even a racist has some good points."

Ironically, *The Last of the Whitfields* is still in print and still selling.

"I like *McBee's Station* better than *The Whitfields*. I think it's a better book. The humor comes out better. . . . I hear from all these people named Whitfield all over the world, as if I'm related to them. These little towns in Georgia, they think it's not fiction. It's fiction, believe me.

"History professors have taken up *The Whitfields* now. I suppose it's the race thing. I'm just puzzled, that's all."

~

More about Elise Sanguinetti

Profile:

Elise Ayers Sanguinetti was born Jan. 26, 1926, in Anniston, Ala., to Harry Mell and Edel Ytterboe Ayers.

Mrs. Sanguinetti's father was owner of the *Anniston Star*, where he served as editor and publisher. She attended St. Olaf College for one year and the University of Oslo for the summer session. She received her bachelor's degree from the University of Alabama, where she studied under creative writing instructor Hudson Strode. Mrs. Sanguinetti married Phillip A. Sanguinetti, also a newspaper man, in 1950. Phillip Sanguinetti is now president of Consolidated Publishing Co., publishers of the *Anniston Star*. Mrs. Sanguinetti worked as a reporter and feature writer for the *Anniston Star* for four years before moving to Pittsburgh, Pa., with her husband. There she began writing short stories. After three years of steady work and much communication with *The New Yorker*, she sold a short story to *Mademoiselle*. The magazine got her an agent who talked Mrs. Sanguinetti into turning the short story into her first novel, *The Last of the Whitfields*. Mrs. Sanguinetti published four novels from 1962 to 1971. She has written more than one hundred short stories and has published many in literary magazines. Mrs. Sanguinetti was at work on a novel in her Anniston home in the fall of 1994.

Works:

McBee's Station, Holt, 1971.
The Dowager, Scribner, 1968.
The New Girl, McGraw, 1964.
The Last of the Whitfields, McGraw, 1962.

Excerpt:

Everybody got up when we came back into the living room and there was this tremendous silence. It was terrible for Miss Esther, I bet, everybody just staring and listening to what she was going to say when she was introduced to Mr. Hopper.

Father introduced her.

"I'm happy to meet you, Mr. Hopper," she said. "I have read your books."

Mr. Hopper nearly passed out with joy. He scratched his laugh and actually put his arm around Miss Esther. I nearly flopped to the floor; nobody in Ashton would dare put their arm around Miss Esther! . . . Then Miss Esther started talking.

"Mr. Hopper just doesn't seem to understand. As you know, Mr. Hopper, we in the South have been poor. Only now are we really recovering from the aftermath of the war. We were never given a Marshall Plan to recover as Germany was. We were completely ravaged by war and we were ravaged in the years following." She was talking like she was making a speech. "But, during all that time, the colored man and the white man in the South grew up together. We had a bond that sustained us — the bond of defeat and even hunger. In most cases we learned to appreciate each other's virtues, to love each other if you will. Also we were striving to uplift ourselves, the colored *and* the white. People in the North are always pointing to the condition of the Negro schools in the South, but many of them are much better than some of the white — to this very day."

Mr. Hopper kind of cleared his throat. "That's interesting, Miss Stein, but then are *you* in favor of integrating the Southern schools?"

"No, I am not."

"Why not?"

"I don't think it would help anything, and I think it would possibly harm some things."

From *The Last of the Whitfields*

Family

Jim Neel

Jim Neel

9

Dennis and Vicki Covington

"

It's not as painful as it used to be," said Mr. Covington. "We depend on each other and trust each other's judgment. In the past we would write it and then show it. Now we talk about it. About the settings, about the whole thing. . . . It's a treasure to have another writer in the house." Said Mrs. Covington: "[Birmingham's] so rich. I can't imagine wanting to leave and go somewhere else. Not when we've got all this wild craziness right here. . . . Those things about us that seem ugly are really interesting and rich and beautiful. . . . I finally feel like I can embrace all that. . . . You've got to be free to tell the truth. . . .

"

91

Family Life

NOVELISTS DENNIS AND VICKI COVINGTON are students of each other.

"Everything we do teaches us," said Mr. Covington. "The thing about Vicki's work that I try to incorporate is the logic of dreams. My work seems too controlled."

"He's compulsive, he's in control," said Mrs. Covington. "That's what I need."

Sitting side-by-side on their sofa — Mr. Covington wearing blue jeans and a rumpled shirt and Mrs. Covington wearing shorts, a T-shirt and bright fingernail polish — they bring to mind a stretch of railroad track in the woods — two rails moving separately and simultaneously away. They work well together. But it wasn't always that way. When they married, they would work separately and show a story only when it was finished.

"It's not as painful as it used to be," said Mr. Covington. "We depend on each other and trust each other's judgment. In the past we would write it and then show it. Now we talk about it. About the settings, about the whole thing. . . . The longer you write and particularly as you get an audience, it doesn't seem to matter quite as much as it used to. I just tear off the *New York Times* stuff and she edits it. It's a treasure to have another writer in the house."

Said Mrs. Covington, smiling: "Sometimes we'll come up with something that really is a good detail and fight over who's going to use it."

About sharing her work in progress with her husband, she said: "I can tell when he's reading it. I can tell by the look on his face that the verdict is not good. . . . All I know is there came this point when we were able to show each other work in progress. We were confident enough about our own work."

Both writers wrote short stories for years before moving to the novel.

"It's important that we're not writing short stories because they're too hard and precise," said Mrs. Covington. "I hope I never write another one as long as I live. It's too painful to do. It's so much harder than a novel."

Said Mr. Covington: "Time is money now, and there's no money in short stories."

Money is a concern — the Covingtons have children and live in a two-story house in Homewood, an upper-middle class Birmingham suburb. Mrs. Covington stays home with the children and writes full time.

"You don't tell yourself what to dream," said Mrs. Covington. "I can't force myself to write anything. If I knew how to write books that would bring me a million dollars, I'd do it."

Both are from the east side of Birmingham, and Birmingham and the surrounding areas are prominent in their work.

Said Mrs. Covington: "[Birmingham's] so rich. I can't imagine wanting to leave and go somewhere else. Not when we've got all this wild craziness right here. New York loves the South. It works in our favor. They want what we got. . . . Those things about us that seem ugly are really interesting and rich and beautiful. If you take racism, it looks so ugly and dark. And you bisect it and look inside and it's so sad and poignant. I finally feel like I can embrace all that. I hate that kind of political correctness [in the portrayal of characters]. You've got to be free to tell the truth . . . It's so strange that this new wave of censorship is coming from the left."

Then Mr. Covington: "Writers have always been subversives."

Mrs. Covington deals with a subdued racism in her second

novel, *Bird of Paradise*, where she has characters who were "in the movement," and the plot involves an elderly woman deciding whether to sell her home to a black-owned company.

"If you have a political agenda, sometimes you forget to tell the story," Mrs. Covington said. "It didn't seem germane to the story to let that intrude on [the lead character and narrator's] voice.... That book was a time when a voice got into me. She (Honey) just talked to me and I wrote it down. It was a pure kind of spiritual experience."

"She literally wrote it as fast as she could write," said Mr. Covington.

"The busier you are, the easier it is to write," she said. "If I have a lot of time, I get paralyzed. I have eighteen months on this contract. It took 6 months to write *Bird of Paradise*, but it took a year to write *A Night Ride Home*. I never know where I'm going from one sentence to the next. About two-thirds or three-quarters of the way there, I know the end. I wrote short stories for eleven years. The first chapter [of *Gathering Home*] was a short story. At heart we'll always be short story writers telling long stories."

"It's hard and exhausting," Mr. Covington said of writing. "It's really a matter of grueling labor."

"I can't work more than two, maybe three hours," Mrs. Covington said. "I write it and clean it up later. I believe it's best to vomit it out and then clean up the mess. I'm horrible; I'll change somebody's eye color or hair color [halfway through the book)."

Mrs. Covington left to tend to their two girls, Ashley and Laura.

"We aren't teaching them to write," Mr. Covington said.

Mrs. Covington returned to the couch for a moment and said: "They want to be involved. We take them on book tours. But they don't like it when we're doing it, writing."

She left again and Mr. Covington talked about his career: "I never had a job in journalism. I came at it ass-backwards. I try to keep them [fiction and journalism] separate in my head as much as

I can. There is a very fine line between the two — fiction and nonfiction. In nonfiction you're capturing more than just the exact words. The kind of journalism I do is like fiction. I have to have both. It keeps me in balance. Reporting gives me a way of relating to people. It's like a social occasion to me. I really get involved in these person's lives."

Even so, facing a deadline is difficult: "When I'm in the middle of a story it feels like I'm gonna die."

Mrs. Covington came back to the couch briefly. One of the girls began to cry as she talked: "I wanted an advance on a book from Simon and Schuster and there were a lot of plot revisions and changes. I was crying and Dennis called. One of the girls answered the phone and told him, 'Mommy's crying because the editor criticized her.'"

She left again, rolling her eyes and smiling, and Mr. Covington continued, above the commotion, to talk about family and the South.

"We [Southerners] are one of the few groups in the country who know who we are. The question that we ask that drives other people crazy is 'Where are you from?' What that really means is 'Who is your Daddy?'"

∾

More about Vicki Covington

Profile:

Vicki Covington was born Vicki Marsh on Oct. 22, 1952, in Birmingham, Ala., to Jack and Katherine Marsh. She was reared in Birmingham, receiving a bachelor of arts in 1974 and a masters of social work in 1976 from the University of Alabama.

In 1977 she married writer and creative writing teacher Dennis Covington. She then began a twelve-year career as a clinical social worker in Alabama. She began publishing short stories in literary magazines in 1981. She published two stories in *The New*

Yorker in 1986. In 1988 she received a National Endowment for the Arts creative writing fellowship and Simon and Schuster published her first novel, *Gathering Home*. She has published two other novels, *Night Ride Home* and *Bird of Paradise*, and was under contract to write a fourth.

Vicki and Dennis Covington have two daughters, Ashley and Laura.

Works:
Night Ride Home, Simon and Schuster, 1992.
Bird of Paradise, Simon and Schuster, 1990.
Gathering Home, Simon and Schuster, 1988.

Excerpt:
Naturally, I called for help and ran, the best I could in that eroding topsoil, to the Family Life Suite (I was wearing tennis shoes), dialed the paramedics, and ran back to Dinah. I didn't know CPR, but it didn't matter. Dinah was gone. I just took the bobby pins from her hair which she'd forgotten to do upon arriving at the cemetery and smoothed the curls, thinking they were too tight. I shouldn't have used rosewater. It didn't matter, in the long run, because Arlene Faucett, Dinah's beautician, with whom she'd set an appointment for the next day, asked to come over to the funeral home and set Dinah's hair for the burial. You might think this peculiar, but I, frankly, was touched. Anyway, I ran my fingers over Dinah's pin curls, buttoned the red cardigan, and shivered a lot because it was cold and I was holding my sister who'd just spoken to me from heaven. I hummed the first hymn that came to mind, which happened to be the one that goes, "Open my eyes that I may see / Glimpses of truth Thou has for me. Place in my hand the wonderful key / That may unclasp and set me free. Silently now, I wait for Thee, / Ready, my God, Thy will to see. / Open my eyes, illumine me, Spirit divine."

The paramedics got there in no time, and they tried to get a sign from her, but to no avail, of course. I stood nearby. It was like watching somebody knead bread.

From *Bird of Paradise*

~

More about Dennis Covington

Profile:

Dennis Covington was born Oct. 30, 1948, in Birmingham, Ala., to Sam and Ellaree Covington. He earned a B.A. in English from the University of Virginia and an M.F.A. from the University of Iowa Writer's Workshop. He began his teaching career in 1974 at Miles College.

In 1977, he married Vicki Marsh, then a social worker, and now a successful novelist. Vicki and Dennis Covington have two daughters, Ashley and Laura.

Mr. Covington also taught at The College of Wooster in Ohio before coming to the University of Alabama at Birmingham in 1978. He has written for the *New York Times*, *Redbook* and *Vogue*. His latest novel, *Lasso the Moon*, and a nonfiction book on snake handlers in the Appalachians entitled *Salvation on Sand Mountain*, were both published in 1995. His first novel, *Lizard*, was adapted for the stage and produced by the Alabama Shakespeare Festival.

Works:

Salvation on Sand Mountain: Snake Handling and Redemption in Southern Appalachia, Addison-Wesley, 1995.

Lasso The Moon, Delacorte Press, 1995.

Lizard, Delacorte Press, 1991.

Excerpt:

The first rocket sounded like a thunderclap. From every corner of the lake women screamed. The rocket flashed once in the air above a twisted plume of smoke, then boomed again louder, and it was dark. A dud, the crowd seemed to moan. I looked back toward the bus and wondered whether the albinos would wet their pants like they had at the rodeo.

It sounded like thunder again, and this time the rocket rose with a hiss, leaving a sparkling trail as thin as an eyelash. There was a pause, a flash of light, and the sky above us opened in green and yellow that showered onto the lake.

"Did you see that?" Simonetti asked.

"I've seen fireworks before," I said, although I hadn't. The air smelled dangerous and sharp. "Over there!" cried boys in the field beyond the lake, their flashlights red in the rolling smoke. They were setting off an entire row, and suddenly the sky rattled with little explosions leading to a huge gold and silver ball that collapsed upon itself.

"What was this lady's name, anyway?" I asked.

"I'll tell you later. Did you see those spinning things?"

Two rockets crossed paths. They exploded like starfish, one on top of the other. For the first time I noticed the sirens and, beneath them, the sound of the Leesville High School Band tuning up. A trombone made a sliding note as another dud fell tumbling into the water. Then the band struck up "Oh, say, can you see . . ." and after a minute people started to sing. It sounded like wind through trees. The rockets came closer together now, a blue one, then crimson and gold, and green. The band and voices went higher, off key, until the field beyond the lake started hissing and sputtering brightly through the smoke. "Take cover!" the boys cried, their flashlights bobbing, and a dozen or more rockets went up all at once. I knew what was coming: "The land of the free . . ." but I'd had it with Simonetti's lies.

"What do you really want out of me?" I said.

He turned just enough so that the whole lit-up sky was reflected in his glasses. "All right, Lizard," he replied. "You win."

He peeled off his moustache and rolled the tip of his nose into a little ball. "There's nothing to be afraid of." He took off his glasses and turned fully to face me.

They were singing, "The home of the brave." I didn't recognize him for a minute, until the play about Treasure Island came back to me. He was Long John Silver, and in the dead silence after the fireworks had ended, I turned around, following his eyes. Parked beside the school bus, underneath the trees, was the actors' truck, its engine ticking, and the woman who had played Jim Hawkins was waiting for me.

From *Lizard*

Courtesy of the Columbus (Ohio) Dispatch

10

E<small>LIZABETH</small> D<small>EWBERRY</small>

I feel my highest obligation to my art and secondly to my family and myself." A gray-haired woman turned to look. "I just feel like my work demands it. If it didn't, I would have children by now. I don't think I could be raising children while I've got these characters in my mind. It's not fully a choice, it's just the way it is. All art is a risk in some sense. All artists are risk-takers. It's not a decison that I make over and over.

99

It's A Risk

ELIZABETH DEWBERRY IS STRONG-WILLED, driven and singular in her ambition. "It takes over my life. I don't know how to write without obsessing over it. My husband understands it. He knows it's something I have to do. . . . When I go long periods without writing I get anxious and depressed. . . . "

Ms. Dewberry talked about herself between sips of Diet Coke in Applebee's in Brookwood Mall in Birmingham. It was February 1994, and she was back in her hometown briefly as part of a month-long book tour for *Break the Heart of Me*. A slight, blonde woman, Ms. Dewberry looks more like a shrinking, straight-laced elementary school teacher than a college professor — until she opens her mouth.

When asked if two years is a long time to focus and write a novel, she replied, curtly: "Why?"

"I don't use an outline. Writing is a real organic process and I keep trying things until I get what seems to be true. [The work in progress] doesn't have any external structure. I have ideas of where I'm trying to get, but I don't know how I'm going to get there. . . . The writing process is something like hearing a tune in the back of your head and trying to pick it out on the piano."

Does the sense that writing somehow controls the writer, that it is mysterious, create doubts that it will continue?

"There's no pressure because I have a lot more support now. I know a lot of writers and I know myself better. I wrote a novel that I'm not going to publish [*The Last Southern Gentleman*], so I know I'm capable of writing things that I know I'm not going to publish. It makes me careful. It makes me scrutinize my work more."

The day before the interview she told a crowd at a reading at the Birmingham library: "I wait until I have someone in my head who needs their story told."

At the restaurant she said: "I start with character. Plot always comes later. The first few months I'm getting to know the person. I keep the characters in my head all the time and then when I get to the end, it's hard to let them go. . . . You get to a certain point where she [the character] feels so real you're really trying to get to know her better. [I] never feel like I'm creating.

"I do a little bit of scholarship, but I don't write short stories, I don't write non-fiction for magazines. I spend a lot of time in revision. . . . The first one hundred pages are by far harder than anything else. That's when I'm trying to figure out what the book is about.

"When I'm writing, I write four, five, six days a week. I can't write erratically . . . Usually I make notes of what I want to do the next day.

"Teaching is clearly secondary to me. I do whatever I can to reduce classes. I never have more than two in a quarter. I like that interaction with colleagues and students. I like the stimulation and nurturing of the university environment. But I'm not going to let teaching keep me from writing."

That view is somewhat ironic considering Ms. Dewberry set out to be a college professor. "Part of the appeal was having summers off to write."

People wandered by the open restaurant inside the mall. Occasionally a comment from Ms. Dewberry would turn a head or stop someone from eating.

"I feel my highest obligation to my art and secondly to my family and myself." A gray-haired woman turned to look. "I just feel like my work demands it. If it didn't, I would have children by now. I don't think I could be raising children while I've got these characters in my mind. It's not fully a choice, it's just the way it is. All art is a risk in some sense. All artists are risk-takers. It's not a decison that I make over and over.

"I'm trying to grow as a writer and trying to push myself to do new things. I hope I'm at the beginning. I'm working on developing *Many Things Have Happened Since He Died* into a one-woman show. I want to write more novels and write better novels."

Ms. Dewberry said she would like to try writing a novel in third person. "First person feels more natural for me. Third person would be more of a challenge."

And: "I'd like to try my hand at writing for the screen. I prefer movies. [I'd like to do it] mostly because I think it might be fun and also because money has something to do with it. In one sense I feel happy with the money I've made, but it's not enough to live off of."

Ms. Dewberry said the book tour is important because it shows her publisher has faith in her work, wants to take part in making her a successful writer.

"Almost every night you go in a bookstore and read from your book and sign. It's tiring. I feel grateful to be doing it. It's important to me. If it didn't happen I'd just keep going.

"I write because I'm trying to make sense out of things. The emotional chords in the novel are the things I care about. I try to correct them, understand them, exorcise them. In a way it works. There's something satisfying about turning an internal conflict into an external entity. . . . I don't think, when I write, in terms of audience and sales."

She also doesn't think in terms of being a Southern writer.

"I don't know how to answer whether the South has influenced my work. I don't want to feel like I'm a regional writer in the sense that you have to be Southern to understand it. I hope the core of that book is about human nature."

Would she consider moving home? Is it important for a region for a writer to choose to live and work there?

"Sometimes it's possible that it would happen. I don't feel an obligation to live my life to shape Birmingham's public image."

Ms. Dewberry said she had begun work on a third novel, this one about a woman who burns her house down while her husband is inside.

"I wanted to write about a woman who empowered herself. For a while I thought it was going to be through witchcraft. . . . The nice thing about writing a novel is you lose those attachments [to sentences or passages of prose]. When I cut something I don't completely delete it from the world. I have eight pages that I loved and wrote six years ago that belong in the novel I'm writing."

At the library, someone asked Ms. Dewberry if she had ever gone to a bookstore and anonymously asked for one of her own books. She laughed. "I've done secret book askings. And they always say, 'We'll be glad to order that for you.'"

❧

More about Elizabeth Dewberry

Profile:

Elizabeth Dewberry was born September 7, 1962, to Jim and Sallie Dewberry in Birmingham, Ala.

She graduated from Vanderbilt University in 1983 with an English and creative writing degree. She earned her Ph.D. in American Literature in 1989 from Emory University. She taught American literature and creative writing in the MFA program at Ohio State University in Columbus, Ohio, through the fall of 1994, when she quit to move to St. Charles, La., to write full time.

Her first novel, *Many Things Have Happened Since He Died*, was published in 1992. Her second, *Break the Heart of Me*, was published in 1994. Ms. Dewberry's move to St. Charles, La., was precipitated by her divorce in 1994 and subsequent plans to marry Robert Olin Butler, a Pulitzer Prize-winning writer.

Works:
Break the Heart of Me, Doubleday, 1994.
Many Things Have Happened Since He Died, Doubleday, 1992.

Awards:
Fellowships from the Alabama Arts Council and the Georgia Council for the Arts.

Excerpt:
So then I hung up the phone and I didn't have any idea what to think and I felt just like when Memaw died, like you're not even upset because you can't really believe what's happened. So I finished making the milkshakes and brought Paw Paw's in to him and drank mine with him but I couldn't think or hear or see or taste anything because I felt like I was far, far away, and I was directing my body to drink that milkshake like by remote control. Then I kissed Paw Paw goodnight and went in the bathroom and washed my face and hands and threw up and brushed my teeth like I always did and went to bed. The only thing different was I got up in the middle of the night and threw up some more, but I didn't think anything of it except good.

And the next morning Paw Paw was dead and the milkshakes were gone and for the first time I noticed that Rouch-Prufe right there on the counter right next to the Slim-fast and I knew what the shepherds felt like when they were sore afraid. I wa so scared my arms hurt.

I kept trying to undo the night before, unraveling everything in my head from the speech to the kiss to the milkshakes to Bo apologizing to the throwing up to Paw Paw dying, and I would have given anything in the world if I could have just made it all not have happened. But of course I couldn't, and I didn't know what I should do and I didn't know what Christ would do or what Amazing Grace would do, but I knew what Memaw would do. Clean up your own mess. So I started cleaning. I put the Roach-Prufe under the sink and I put the Slim-fast back in the pantry and washed both our glasses out with soap and put them in the dishwasher and poured some detergent in there and turned it on even though it wasn't half full and I knew Uncle Mull would complain stop wasting electricity but I wanted to get my fingerprints off the glass and I wanted the Roach-Prufe not to be there, never to have been there, and all I could think was run the dishwasher.

From *Break the Heart of Me*

The Montgomery Advertiser

11

HELEN NORRIS BELL

The question of where does it all come from fascinates me. I think it comes from outside. . . . The paranormal enters into writing. When you are writing creatively, you know things you could not know. . . . I think you do get into other people's minds somehow when you are doing this. You are trying so hard and you are pushing against some membrane and it breaks and you know things. I think writing is an adventure of the mind and spirit and you never come out the same as you went in.

"

Where It Comes From

HELEN NORRIS BELL SPENT MOST OF AN April evening trying to understand the origin of her fiction. She talked and thought on the screened back porch of her ranch-style house in Montgomery. She thought about it in her spacious living room decorated in a low, long style popular in the sixties. She thought and talked about it in the narrow foyer and outside on her driveway.

"The question of where does it all come from fascinates me. I think it comes from outside. . . . The paranormal enters into writing. When you are writing creatively, you know things you could not know. . . . I think you do get into other people's minds somehow when you are doing this. You are trying so hard and you are pushing against some membrane and it breaks and you know things. I think writing is an adventure of the mind and spirit and you never come out the same as you went in.

"If you have a problem and try to write about it creatively, you are forced to empathize. You've got to empathize with all kinds of characters. You don't know how men feel, but you have to learn how they feel. You get better comprehension of other people. I never write about myself and I never write about people I know. . . . Writing comes from inspiration from outside myself. I don't know where it comes from. [Readers] can't conceive of it not coming from within you."

She told a story about the writing of *Walk with the Sickle Moon*.

Having never been to France, where the story is set, Mrs. Bell was relying on a French friend to offer details about landscape and customs. However, by the end of *Walk with the Sickle Moon*, Mrs. Bell said that without the aid of her friend, she had described perfectly an area of France with a particularly unusual landscape.

Mrs. Bell narrowed her small eyes and smiled. "It's fun to live with a creative mind. I think you have to be very sane when you're doing something like this. When the pressure is put on me I will collapse physically, but not emotionally. I'm just your average garden variety uptight old woman."

Maybe not.

"I have had three different periods of my life when I've written, and others when I didn't write. If you're a woman you have other things to do, like raise children. Working as a writer conflicts with being a woman. A man can say, I'm going to write. A woman can't do that. She can't separate herself from her children. They sense when they're very little that they don't want you to do this because your attention is diverted from them. They will do everything they can to interrupt you. My son to this day doesn't want me to write."

Later, standing on her driveway under a huge oak, Mrs. Bell, small, conservative, neatly dressed, talked about her children. She talked about a daughter who was killed in 1958 and how during the days leading up to the anniversary of her child's death, Mrs. Bell still feels odd and depressed. Then she talked of her two sons.

"Once I was writing and I noticed my son in the yard. He had gone into a stage where he was trying to build his muscles. He was running around and around lifting a pick over his head. He told me I should stop writing. I asked him what should I do and he said I should do something important like build my muscles."

Another son is an English teacher who does not like to read his mother's work. "I even dedicated one of the books to him," Mrs. Bell said, turning her palms toward the night sky.

Mrs. Bell talks naturally, like an actress in a one-woman show.

Her life pours forth, the tales of her time on this earth rhythmic, deftly chosen for the moment.

"I don't take myself seriously. I take life seriously and others seriously and writing seriously. I write humorous stories, but no one wants to publish them. I think I've just got this great sense of humor."

Earlier, on her porch, cinching her sweater tighter around her shoulders, she told of traveling to Washington, D.C., as a nominee for the PEN Faulkner Award.

"Here was this room full of people who had paid thirty dollars to listen to us read and William Gaddis refused to read. He harangued the crowd for his five minutes about how writers should be read and not heard and he had this elaborate theory. I was next. I got up and said, 'I do have the courage to read to you after what I just heard.' The crowd howled with laughter. They had books on sale and my books sold out after the reading. That was because I was nice to them."

The night air turned cool on the back porch and Mrs. Bell moved into the living room among orderly stacks of books and magazines.

"When I was teaching at Huntingdon I couldn't think of one thing to write about. If you try to teach creatively, it saps you. A colleague of mine would say, 'Helen, if we just sold blouses then at the end of the day we could write.'

"As soon as I quit teaching, all of these things started coming to me. I have a long list of things I want to write and I get frustrated. Now I'm writing poetry. I've never thought of myself as a poet. I can't tell if they're any good. They don't seem to me to be all that good. I have become a poem machine. I want to go back to writing stories, and I can't stop writing these stupid poems. The charm of a poem is that you can get it over. You can get the thing whole in a relatively short period of time. It takes quite a bit longer to do a short story. It takes a matter of weeks and sometimes months. You keep going back to it and back to it and rewriting.

HELEN NORRIS BELL

"It took me twenty years to write that story," she said of "Starwood," collected in the book *The Christmas Wife*. "I just couldn't figure out how it was going to end. At first I was going to have him praying. But having God step in and solve the problems is a cop out.

"When I write, I hear the words in my head first and I put them down the way I heard them. If I'm working on a novel, I take the passages that come to me vividly. I have written scenes first that were used last. Sooner or later I make an outline. I've found that if you make an outline too early it will kill the spontaneity."

Spontaneity . . .

"I write just any old time that I have time to do it. I have a tablet by my bed and I write things in the dark. I don't turn on my light. Sometimes I can't read it and sometimes I write over other things. . . .

"I love to write in my nighty."

∾

More about Helen Norris Bell

Profile:

Helen Norris Bell was born June 22, 1916, in Miami. Her parents, Elmer W. and Louise Brown Norris, moved soon after to the family farm near Montgomery, and Helen was reared there. She attended public schools in Montgomery and graduated from Sidney Lanier High School in 1934.

Helen Norris received her A.B. from the University of Alabama in 1938. She was the first of Hudson Strode's students to earn an M.A. with a novel instead of a thesis. That novel, *Something More Than Earth*, was published the same year, 1940.

She also married Thomas Reuben Bell in 1940. They divorced and Mrs. Bell enrolled in Duke University's graduate school in 1965. She joined the English faculty at Huntingdon College in Montgomery in 1966. Although she wrote no new fiction during

113

her tenure at Huntingdon, she published some previously written work. She taught thirteen years before resigning to write full time.

Works:

The Burning Glass (collected short stories), Louisiana State University Press, 1992.

Walk with the Sickle Moon (a novel), Birch Lane Press, 1989.

Water Into Wine (collected short stories), University of Illinois Press, 1988.

The Christmas Wife (collected short stories), University of Illinois Press, 1985.

More Than Seven Watchmen (a novel), Zondervan Press, 1985.

For the Glory of God (a novel), Macmillan, 1958.

Something More Than Earth (a novel), Atlantic/Little Brown and Company, 1940.

Awards:

The O. Henry Prize in 1984, 1985, 1987, 1991; Andrew Lytle awards in 1984, 1987; Pushcart Prize, 1991; PEN Women's Award for Best Novel, 1989.

Excerpt:

His name was Tanner, a reasonable man in his early sixties, desiring peace, a measure of joy, and reassurance. All that was submerged. The tip of the iceberg was a seasoned smile that discouraged excesses and a way of looking, "That's fine, but not today." His marriage had fitted him like a glove, but now his wife Florence was dead for three years. And so it came to pass that Christmas was a problem.

Not a large problem, but one that niggled when the weather turned and got a little worse with blackbirds swarming in the elm trees, on the move. And here he was looking out at the falling leaves, chewing his November turkey in a restaurant down the block, and going nowhere. Except to his son's in California (Christmas with palm trees!), to his daughter-in-law with the fugitive eyes and his grandsons bent on concussions, riding their wagons down the stairs at dawn, whaling the daylights out of their toys. During the long, safe years of their marriage his hand had been firmly, as they say, on the helm. He had been in control. It alarmed him that now he was not in control, even of his holidays, especially Christmas. A courtly man with a sense of tradition, he liked his Christmases cast in the mold, which is to say he liked them the way they had always been.

Now, the best thing about Thanksgiving was its not being Christmas. It held Christmas at bay. But then the days shortened and the wind swept them into the gutter along with the leaves. And it rained December.

"The Christmas Wife," from *The Christmas Wife*

Mark Gooch

12

MARY WARD BROWN

I don't ever know if it's good. I don't think anything I've ever written is very good, actually. It's just . . . It's just not great. I want to make it a work of art, something that will stand up. It's like a vase that's right. It's something you can look at every day and it will be pleasing. You hope you'll write something better than you've done before. I have readers and I'm always hoping someone will say, 'This is the best thing you've ever done.' But they never say that. . . . It really helps to have a good reader.

99

Just Fortune

MARY WARD BROWN HAS LIVED TWO LIVES: "It got obsessive. I just wanted to write fiction all the time. Here was my husband trying to run the farm. I even had an agent back then, but it wasn't right. If I had been making money it would have been different.

"I didn't write for twenty-five years . . . I stopped because of my family. It did take away [from writing time]. The great women writers, some of them were married, but they didn't have children. I wouldn't have done it differently. It was my duty to look after my family.

"Women are going to learn to their sorrow that they can't do both. They can't do everything. Children being raised in daycare, I wonder how they are going to fare in the world. I think women have a built-in biological destiny to bear and raise children.

"That was just fortune with me, I guess. I did not write when I was full of strength and words and could write with ease. I never was a fast writer. I could write a story in three months. . . . [Now] at the point of a pistol I couldn't write a story in less than six months. I think if I had more talent I could write faster. I have to struggle with the sentences and move them around and change words around. . . . But that was just the way the cookie crumbled for me."

Mrs. Brown, in her mid-seventies, is a slight, prim woman. She has a genteel manner, and her immaculate dress is conservative. She lives in the tree-shrouded country home in which she was reared. Inside, amid the dark, heart pine walls, Mrs. Brown is all energy, all concentration. During a 1992 interview she moved excitedly from room to room, up- stairs and down, picking up books of fiction and scholarship, talking, pointing, reading. In a 1994 telephone conversation she laughed at herself regularly, chiding herself for being too serious.

"The creative process starts with a germ and you manipulate it with the writing. It could be a bit of conversation. Something gets your attention and it doesn't go away. It begins to gather information around it. [Writing] is something you're born doing. People who don't write are struck by things and they remember them. But they don't come out. If you write fiction, you want to let it out. I think you wonder how other human beings react. I think it's a search to see the meaning of what's stuck in your mind.

"I'm a better writer now than I was at sixty. I've learned how to handle the material better. I don't know why I think that. I would think anybody who worked as hard as I did for all those years would have learned a lot about writing fiction.

"I don't ever know if it's good. I don't think anything I've ever written is very good, actually. It's just . . . it's just not great. I want to make it a work of art, something that will stand up. It's like a vase that's right. It's something you can look at every day and it will be pleasing. You hope you'll write something better than you've done before. I have readers and I'm always hoping someone will say, 'This is the best thing you've ever done.' But they never say that . . . It really helps to have a good reader.

"I don't know how good a judge I am. I think what I do is honest. I try to tell the truth and I think I do that in my own simple way. Before I send a story out I have done the absolute best I can do with that piece of work. It's an honest effort."

After a pause: "I've never thought mine were finished. I always thought I could go back and do a little something to them. . . . I worked on "A New Life" for three different publications and I think finally it's about what it should be.

"I want the reader to feel something. I'd like for them to hurt a little. Style has a lot to do with getting them to feel that jolt. Style is over and beyond technique. I've often wondered if my style is distinctive.

"I find I know some good words, but the words I tend to use are simple. I'm reading Carmack McCarthy, and when I read him I have to have a dictionary and a notebook. I have to look up so many words. I know well that nobody would read my stuff if they had to look up words. . . . I've learned a lot about grammar since I've been writing fiction. You need to know the rules of grammar. I've had to learn that the hard way. I'd try to be clear and realize it wasn't clear because of a grammatical error. . . . The mechanics are necessary. If you can't handle the mechanics, you can't let the story shine forth."

Learning to handle the mechanics takes effort. "I got up at five o'clock this morning and stopped around nine. I go straight to work when I get up. I find that if I get dressed or straighten the house I get side-tracked. I work in bed first and go over what I did the day before. Then in the afternoon I put it on the computer. I don't do much in longhand except to make changes.

"I do sentences twenty four times sometimes. I do them over and over to get the greatest effect. It's hard to cut. No cuts ever get used. Sometimes I go back and think, 'that was a good paragraph.' I just ruthlessly cut them. In a short story you have to be ruthless. . . . The story I'm working on now [after a two-year effort] was never sent out because it wasn't right. I just saw a whole little section that I liked and worked on and did research on, but it didn't belong. When you start out you have so much material to work with. You can look back and to the sides. There was so much material that I would write off in tangents and then I had to cut, cut back.

"I haven't had a hard time working with editors. I haven't sold a lot of stories to editors who want to do things to my work. The literary magazines grant you your integrity. I sold a story to the

Three Penny Review and she didn't use it for six months. After six months I called her and asked to make changes. She said, 'Let's see.' Most of my changes went in. Like this new story I have just done. If it could have been improved, I would have improved it."

In the 1992 interview, Mrs. Brown sat at her kitchen table and talked of her work living after she is gone. "It's so risky to try to write fiction. I was fifty-three when my husband died. I could have done something that I knew would be productive. I could have helped people live. Five years from the time I'm dead my book could be [in a bin at Goodwill]. I could have lost my gamble that I could do anything that could amount to anything."

Other comments from that day:

❧

"I don't put all that [symbolism] in on purpose. A lot of it just comes from your subconscious as you learn about the character. When I write stories I see things I have written and wonder where that came from. The reader brings so much to a story. If it is real, it can have all those meanings."

❧

"Writing is not fun. It's a deep pleasure. Is pleasure the word? Maybe a need. It's not recreation. It's hard work. Always a search, a desperate search to give form to experience. Autobiography is not fiction. You have to be detached from your experience. If the author's ego is in there it ruins it. The experience has to be reprocessed through your imagination."

❧

"It's hard to write fiction. It takes physical strength. Sometimes I'm so tired when I write a story I think I've aged five years. . . . I eat right and I try to walk every afternoon. Old age is a new territory, and it's not good. But I don't think about that. I just want to write more stories."

❧

More about Mary Ward Brown

Profile:

Mary Thomas Ward Brown was born in 1917 in Perry County, Ala., to Thomas Ira and Mary Fitts Ward.

She grew up on the family's farm in Hamburg and attended Judson College in nearby Marion. There she majored in journalism and worked as the college's public relations director for a year after her graduation. She married Charles Kirtley Brown and moved with him to Auburn, where he was public relations director at the university. They had a son, Kirtley, in 1942 and the family moved back to Hamburg in 1943 to run the farm after Mrs. Brown's father died. With the encouragement of a sister-in-law, Margery Finn Brown, who wrote for popular magazines, Mrs. Brown began taking writing courses in Tuscaloosa. She published a story in 1957 and another in 1958, but had to give up writing because it was too time-consuming. Mrs. Brown deferred to the interest of her family. She began writing again in 1970 when her husband died. She published a short story, "Amaryllis," in *McCall's* in 1978. She continued to publish in prestigious literary journals and in 1986, eleven stories were published in a collection entitled *Tongues of Flame*. In her middle seventies, Mrs. Brown continues to write short stories in hopes of publishing another collection.

Works:

Tongues of Flame, Pocket Books, 1986.

Awards:

1987 PEN/Ernest Hemingway Foundation Award for best first fiction and the 1987 Alabama Library Association Award for *Tongues of Flame*.

Excerpt:

He took a seat on the sofa, in front of which the plant stood on a low table from which he and Margaret used to serve demitasses or port after dinner. They had never cared much for society, but entertained when they had to and enjoyed having friends for dinner until her heart problems stopped even that.

In the handsome room, in an artificial light, the amaryllis seemed to have taken on a glamour, like a beautiful girl all dressed up for the evening. All dressed up and no place to go, he thought.

The strange thing was, he'd never "felt" anything for a plant before. On the contrary, he'd dismissed them all as more or less inanimate like potatoes and turnips, not animate in the way of cats and birds. He had bought dozens of hospital chrysanthemums, often delivering them himself in their foil wrapping and big bows, but they had seemed more artificial than real.

The amaryllis was different, entirely. He liked just being with it. Because of its size, he supposed, it seemed to have individuality, and then he had watched it grow daily, with his naked eye. Looking at the blooms, he thought of words like *pure* and *noble*, and old lines of poetry like "Euclid alone has looked on *Beauty* bare."

In return, the plant seemed neither friendly nor unfriendly. It was simply there in all its glory, however fleeting. It was the fleetingness, he thought, that put on the pressure.

He took off his glasses, dropped them in his shirt pocket, and rubbed a hand across both eyes. Then he turned off the lights, one by one.

"The Amaryllis," from *Tongues of Flame*

Jackson Clarion-Ledger

13

MARGARET WALKER ALEXANDER

"

I'm not only a black woman. I'm poor in the needs of the world. I came back to teach [at Jackson State University in Jackson, Miss.] in the South in 1949. I had five classes with fifty or more students in each class. How I managed to grade those papers, raise four children, take care of a disabled husband and write. . . . It was next to impossible. I was living under very difficult conditions. Making a living was what I had to do. People do what they want to do. You don't find the time [to write], you make the time. I'd find myself writing at night and on weekends and holidays.

"

Making the Time

MRS. ALEXANDER LOOKED TOWARD THE sliding glass door as she sat quietly in the hot, un-airconditioned room at the back of her aging house in a predominantly black section of Jackson. In the room were pictures — most old black and white photos of groups of blacks at awards ceremonies. There was a large color picture of Jesse Jackson next to the fireplace. It was noisy outside; children were playing. Her small grandson peeked in. She waved to him.

"I think my writing was always influenced by my being a black woman, because that's what I knew. If you look back, there are three prongs to all my writing. One is the vision. I envision a world where humanity counts more than race. Two is the historical line. The work is the historical background of black people. Three is revolution. I believe that our society has to be changed from a racist, fascist and sexist society. I believe change must take place.

"The forces that have been against us keep us looking at the differences more than the likenesses [between different races]," she said, patting the cane next to the wing-back chair in which she sat. "Any black person living in the South went through a lot of things that are not good. But I cannot let them corrode me inside.

"I'm not only a black woman. I'm poor in the needs of the world. I came back to teach [at Jackson State University in Jackson, Miss.] in the South in 1949. I had five classes with fifty or more students in each class. How I managed to grade those pa-

pers, raise four children, take care of a disabled husband and write
. . . it was next to impossible. I was living under very difficult conditions. Making a living was what I had to do. People do what they
want to do. You don't find the time [to write], you make the time.
I'd find myself writing at night and on weekends and holidays."

She grinned, cut her eyes, and said: "I've always been ambitious; very competitive and ambitious. I knew from the time I was
eight years old exactly what I wanted to do. I didn't live within the
narrow world of my physical parameters. Don't tell me what I
can't do.

"When Saul Bellow got the Nobel Prize I felt bad. We were
the same age, had the same teacher. And when I see what he did, I
feel embarrassed because I have not done what he did. My daughter said to me that he was at one of those schools that lobby for the
Nobel Prize every year. I taught all my life in the South for my
people. My students are my great reward. Teaching is a reward in
itself. I enjoyed the classroom.

"If I hadn't taught I don't think I would have written any more
than I have done. I made a contribution teaching. I taught people
how to learn, how to do research. When I went to Jackson State
there was not a single Ph.D. there. By the time I left, most people
on the administrative staff were people I had taught who had gone
on to get their Ph.D."

Mrs. Alexander is feeble; she walks with a cane. Her thin fingers shake when she lifts her hands to make a point during conversation. But she still controls a room. She is at once a mother, a
young woman reading poems on a nationwide tour, a child watching the iron-ore dust-covered men return from work in Birmingham mines.

"I realize to a certain extent I had great advantages. My parents were intellectuals. They were a part of that rising black bour-
geoisie. When I went to Chicago, I couldn't convince them [her
contemporaries in the Works Progress Authority Writer's Project]
I had never picked cotton. In New Orleans we lived in the univer-

sity section. The school where my mother and father taught was on St. Charles Avenue. Our house was in the only block of black people in that section. We lived among the white people in an upper-class section. I grew up in that. I went to school where my parents were teaching."

Such a life was not always hers, however.

"When my father was teaching in Meridian, [Miss.,] he told my mother not to go to town without him. My mother went one day by herself and was scared to death. You were not allowed to touch certain things. My mother hated Meridian. My father, if he had stayed, could have been in charge of the school. She said, 'What time does the train leave?'"

So, when Mrs. Alexander was eight her family moved back to her native Birmingham.

"Father worked two years in public schools in Birmingham. The police had ways of going around in the black community, and they would shine a light into the houses looking for whiskey. My mother was scared to death they were going to come into the house. We didn't have any whiskey inside. I went to school in a one-room school in Birmingham called Slater. [Black schools] were in small, one-room houses. It was a disgrace to see those black children piled into those one-room houses."

She tells of being older, in high school in New Orleans.

"I was just fifteen then. The teacher told [her parents] to 'get Margaret to another school.' Some Jewish people took some of my poetry to a professor at Tulane, but I couldn't walk on that campus. The black people who could were cooks and maids. It was bad everywhere. Racism is not stronger and more venemous in the South. It's all over the country. I think it's in New York and Boston. I've lived those places. I don't want to go there.

"At Yale they asked me why couldn't I get a job and stay there? Why would I want to be a second-class citizen [living in the South]? They said I could live in Harlem. I thought Harlem was a garbage dump."

It was her talent as a writer that led Mrs. Alexander out of the South for a time. Langston Hughes visited New Orleans while she lived there and read some of her poems. "He told my parents, 'You should get her out of the South so she can be a writer.' My father was a Methodist minister, and he could get a rebate if he sent me to Northwestern. So, I went to Northwestern."

After graduating she took a job writing for the Works Progress Administration in Chicago, where she met Richard Wright. They had an intense friendship which ended suddenly in 1939 in New York when Mrs. Alexander visited there.

"I was young and I thought the world of that man, but there was not even a kiss between us. We were working together and helping each other."

Wright had moved to New York, where he was becoming successful. He asked Mrs. Alexander to visit him there. The abrupt end to their friendship had been a mystery until Mrs. Alexander said, nearly fifty-five years later: "What do you think it means when you open a hotel door and see a man in bed with another man? He thought I would tell. I never told. I was twenty-three years old, how much did I know? I had to be an old woman to understand what was going on in New York."

Her understanding of the world came at a price. Mrs. Alexander believes Alex Haley and an editor from *Playboy* stole from *Jubilee*, her book about the black American experience beginning with slavery, to write *Roots*. She sued Haley and lost. She also had a protracted court battle with Wright's widow before she could publish her biography of Wright entitled *Richard Wright: Daemonic Genius*.

"There are [parts of] four hundred pages of *Roots* that were taken out of *Jubilee*. They made a movie in Hollywood in 1974, and they were holding copies of *Jubilee* while they were making the movie. . . . There are bits of one hundred books in *Roots*. Haley was very crafty. . . . I was thrown out of court. I couldn't understand what I had done to undergo what I got from people who said I was just jealous or envious of that man's money.

"For years I was very upset over Haley. Finally, in 1985 I came down to this room and sat down and I said, 'Now Lord, I understand.' I put that knowledge [legal knowledge acquired in her battle over *Roots*] to use so I could get *Richard Wright* published. Richard Wright's widow spent a hundred thousand dollars to [try to] keep that book from being published."

That battle was not the first in Mrs. Alexander's literary life. And it certainly wasn't the most difficult.

"It's very hard for a white man with talent to get published. It's harder for a white woman. It's harder for a black man. But it's easier for him than for a black woman because a black woman is at the bottom of the ladder. It was hard for me to get somebody to read my stuff and very hard to get it published. A black girl in the South wanting to write books . . . it was a joke.

"I started writing when I was very young. When I was eleven years old I started writing poetry. I thought it was hard to do. I wrote every day of my adolescence. It's easy to read a poem. I began reading a lot of black writers. The Harlem rennaissance was very much in vogue at that time. Langston Hughes was the leading writer. So, I was interested in poetry.

"It took me a long time to learn the technique of fiction. I have three more pieces to write to show I understand the technique — if I live.

"In poetry you soon run out of rhymes. I learned that there are three things that every poem needs — pictures, music and meaning. Music doesn't have to be rhymed lines."

Her greatest fiction accomplishment is *Jubilee*, published in 1966. It is the story of Mrs. Alexander's great-grandmother who was a slave and eventually won freedom. The book offers a rich background on the dynamics of the South before and after the Civil War.

"I finished *Jubilee* when I was forty-five. Ten years went into serious research, reading Civil War novels, history books, studying maps. I became saturated with the period. I tried to do three or four things. I tried to show what caused the war, the role the black people played in the war and the effect of the war on the country.

"For a black book to stay in print twenty-five years is unusual. *Jubilee* has had forty-five printings. To think about how many people have seen this book would be great — if I weren't so ambitious.

"I used to work every day from 9 a.m. to 11 a.m. It took a year to get the first novel down. Now I'm old and sick and sometimes I don't work for weeks at a time. . . .

"I wanted to have a profession and live a life according to my ideals and standards. I also wanted a family."

So, Margaret Walker Alexander, nearly eighty, after raising four children, after teaching at the writer's workshop at the University of Iowa, after traveling the country reading her poetry, after spending more than thirty years teaching in historically black schools in her native South, has one last ambition.

"I'd rather be remembered as a poet. Being a poet is a great thing. I would like my epitaph to read, 'Here lies Margaret Walker, poet and dreamer. She tried to make her life a poem.'"

∾

More about Margaret Walker Alexander

Profile:

Margaret Abigail Walker Alexander was born July 7, 1915, in Birmingham, Ala., to Sigismund Constantine Walker, a West Indian immigrant, a teacher and minister of the Methodist Episcopal Church, and Marion Dozier, a music teacher.

Mrs. Alexander [who writes under her maiden name of Walker] graduated from Gilbert Academy in New Orleans at the age of fifteen. She entered Northwestern University in Illinois in 1932. Mrs. Alexander graduated from Northwestern in 1935 and went to work on the WPA Writer's Project in Chicago. It was during this time that her famous friendship with Richard Wright blossomed. She went to the University of Iowa in the fall of 1939 and completed her master's degree there in 1940. After several teaching appointments she returned to the University of Iowa and completed her Ph.D. in 1965. Mrs. Alexander began teaching at Livingstone College in Salisbury, N.C., in 1941. She then went to West Virginia State College, where she taught the academic year 1942-43. In 1943 she became a lecturer with the National Concert and Artists Corporation. She held that job until 1948. In 1949, wanting to move close to her mother and father, she began teaching at Jackson State University. Except for brief periods of study, she remained at Jackson State until her retirement.

Mrs. Alexander married Firnist James Alexander. They had three children.

Works:

How I Wrote Jubilee and Other Essays on Life and Literature, The Feminist Press, 1990.

This Is My Century: New and Collected Poems, University of Georgia Press, 1989.

Richard Wright: Daemonic Genius, Amistad, 1988.

October Journey, Broadside Press, 1973.

How I Wrote Jubilee, Third World Press, 1972.

Prophets for a New Day, Broadside Press, 1970.

Jubilee (a novel), Houghton Mifflin, 1966.

For My People, Yale University Press, 1942.

Awards:

Yale Series Younger Poets Award for *For My People*, 1942; the Rosenwald Fellowship in 1944 and the Ford Fellowship at Yale University during the 1953-54 academic year. Her first novel, *Jubilee*, published in 1966, was the winner of a Houghton Mifflin Fellowship Award.

Excerpt:

FOR MY PEOPLE

For my people everywhere singing their slave songs
 repeatedly: their dirges and their ditties and their blues
 and jubilees, praying their prayers nightly to an
 unknown god, bending their knees humbly to an
 unseen power;

For my people lending their strength to the years, to the
 gone years and the now years and the maybe years,
 washing ironing cooking scrubbing sewing mending
 hoeing plowing digging planting pruning patching
 dragging along never gaining never reaping never
 knowing and never understanding;

For my playmates in the clay and dust and sand of Alabama
 backyards playing baptizing and preaching and doctor
 and jail and soldier and school and mama and cooking
 and playhouse and concert and store and hair and Miss
 Choomby and company;

For the cramped bewildered years we went to school to learn
 to know the reasons why and the answers to and the
 people who and the places where and the days when, in
 memory of the bitter hours when we discovered we
 were black and poor and small and different and nobody
 cared and nobody wondered and nobody understood;

For the boys and girls who grew in spite of these things to
    be man and woman, to laugh and dance and sing and
    play and drink their wine and religion and success, to
    marry their playmates and bear children and then die
    of consumption and anemia and lynching;

For my people thronging 47th Street in Chicago and Lenox
    Avenue in New York and Rampart Street in New
    Orleans, lost disinherited dispossessed and happy
    people filling the cabarets and taverns and other
    people's pockets needing bread and shoes and milk and
    land and money and something — something all our own;

For my people walking blindly spreading joy, losing time
    being lazy, sleeping when hungry, shouting when
    burdened, drinking when hopeless, tied, and shackled
    and tangled among ourselves by the unseen creatures
    who tower over us omnisciently and laugh;

For my people blundering and groping and floundering in
    the dark of churches and schools and clubs and
    societies, associations and councils and committees and
    conventions, distressed and disturbed and deceived and
    devoured by money-hungry glory-craving leeches,
    preyed on by facile force of state and fad and novelty, by
    false prophet and holy believer;

For my people standing staring trying to fashion a better way
    from confusion, from hypocrisy and misunderstanding,
    trying to fashion a world that will hold all the people,

all the faces, all the adams and eves and their countless
generations;

Let a new earth rise. Let another world be born. Let a
bloody peace be written in the sky. Let a second
generation full of courage issue forth; let a people
loving freedom come to growth. Let a beauty full of
healing and a strength of final clenching be the pulsing
in our spirits and our blood. Let the martial songs be
written, let the dirges disappear. Let a race of men now
rise and take control.

Career

The Birmingham Post-Herald

14

HARRY MIDDLETON

"

It's not a romantic existence. People think that if you write books you're rich. But for the average American writer it's not like that at all. It's all check-to-check, month-to-month.

"

The Chance to Work

"I HARBOR THIS NOTION; IT'S THAT I COULD BE of help," said Harry Middleton July 24, 1993, just four days before he died from a massive heart attack while swimming. Mr. Middleton, forty-three, suffered from clinical depression. He was bitter about being fired in 1990 from Southern Progress. He tried, but never got another significant full-time journalism job, so he worked on a garbage truck and swept floors to help support his wife and two children.

He struggled through each day to get to midnight, to get to his notebooks. From midnight to 4:00 a.m. he sat in his cramped study at the top of the stairs and wrote. Because his work was full of fly fishing and hunting and the earth, Mr. Middleton was considered an outdoor writer.

"Fish and streams and mountains are just the background to talk about what I want to talk about. Fly fishing is more than the sum of its parts, it's a connection with the natural world, a world that we used to be a part of. I don't think too much about other worlds, other heavens. This is it."

Thus the title of his first book, *The Earth Is Enough*. That book is a story about growing up, about kindness and love and discipline and humor. In the book, a twelve-year-old boy [Mr. Middleton] is sent to live with his grandfather and great-uncle on a subsistence farm in the Ozark Mountains while his father, a career soldier, serves in Vietnam in the early sixties. The book is jammed with bizarre characters: a crazy Indian bootlegger who is brilliantly insulting, a wine-drinking suspiciously philosophical preacher, two eighty-year-old renaissance men who read Darwin and Plato and discuss modern novels.

Mr. Middleton swore all of it was true.

"I've been blessed to run into the most unusual people. People you meet — waitresses in little cafes and people you meet on trails — are truly mysterious."

Perhaps too mysterious.

In *The Bright Country*, released a couple of months after his death, he wrote of giving Don Logan, former CEO of the Southern Progress Corporation, a fly fishing lesson the morning of the day Logan fired him. "We laughed and laughed," said Mr. Middleton. "We were like long-lost childhood buddies."

In conversation, he often referred to Southern Progress as Never-Never Land, and he wrote in the dedication of *The Bright Country*: "To everyone back in Never-Never Land, back in paradise / OLLIE-OLLIE-OXEN-FREE."

After he was fired, Mr. Middleton went to work in Colorado, where he was overcome by depression. "I woke up on the floor of an unfurnished apartment in Denver." He then began seeing a psychiatrist who "finally found the correct drug to keep my chemicals in line."

Mr. Middleton said that after he lost the job in Colorado he took the medicine when he could afford it. For two years before his death, he slept just three or four hours a day and found his solace dulling pencils on composition notebooks which he bought in bulk because they were cheaper that way.

"The chance to write is what I look forward to. Getting in here is such a relief. I have no trouble shifting gears. I've never had a problem with blocks. My problem is getting me to stop. I like doing books so much because there are no borders. If you are writing a magazine article and go on a ten-page tangent you are in deep shit. That's not the case with writing books. All my books are essentially the same story over and over. The mine never runs out for me. I've left out more than I've ever put in.

"Creative non-fiction is a lot like fiction. You employ some of the same elements. Truth is truth."

Mr. Middleton's truth was hard. His mother, whom he described as "a heavy reader, an interesting, eccentric woman," died young from a brain tumor after battling depression for years. He said of his father: "He is a nice guy. I don't know him on a real deep level. My father doesn't like what I do. He's not a big fan. He was never around. He was always off doing what combat soldiers do.

"I never planned to be a writer [as a child]. I started keeping journals. I started writing stuff like bits and pieces of conversation, the description. Taking into account the world around me."

He crossed his thick arms over his belly.

"I have my addictions. I think writing itself is a terrible addiction. You've got to keep writing. Let it rip. Go with it. Go anywhere. You'd be surprised where writing will take you. It's a tough thing to do. The best writers are the ones who have the ability to break all the rules, become a vessel, start pouring things out. It's a destructive process.

"It's not a romantic existence. People think that if you write books you're rich. But for the average American writer it's not like that at all. It's check-to-check, month-to-month." He said he got five-thousand dollar advances for his books and he never made a royalty.

Talk of money takes the conversation on a philosophical turn and that, as usual, leads to trout.

"Trout don't adapt. They have parameters. In terms of evolution, they're not a very successful fish. You can stock trout, but those essential wild populations; those are the ones everyone is after. They're not like us, where the soul's for sale."

~

More about Harry Middleton

Profile:

The late Harry F. Middleton was born Dec. 28, 1949, in Frankfurt, Germany to Col. (Ret.) H.F. Middleton and Donna Middleton.

Mr. Middleton earned a B.A. in history from Northwestern State University in Louisiana in 1972. He earned an M.A. in American Western History from Louisiana State University in 1974. In 1975 he began a five-year stint with the U.S. Geological Survey in research. It was during that time that he began to write freelance outdoor and humor articles for Louisiana newspapers and magazines. He had a column in the *Morning Advocate* in Baton Rouge, La. Mr. Middleton went to work for *Southern Living* as an outdoor writer in 1983. He left *Southern Living* in 1990 after publishing his first book, *The Earth Is Enough*. After that he worked at the *Rocky Mountain News* as a feature writer for five months before returning to his Hoover, Ala., home, where he wrote creative nonfiction books and magazine and newspaper travel and fishing articles. Mr. Middleton worked numerous odd jobs, including garbage collection for Jefferson County, in an attempt to support his family while he wrote.

He was married to Marcy D. Middleton and they had two sons, Travis and Sean.

He died July 28, 1993.

Works:

The Bright Country, Simon and Schuster, 1993.
Rivers of Memory, Pruett Publishing Co., 1993.
The Starlight Creek Angling Society, Simon and Schuster, 1992.
On the Spine of Time, Simon and Schuster, 1991.
The Earth is Enough, Simon and Schuster, 1989.

Excerpt:

As it turned out, Fairplay was a town I could not have passed up, even if Odell Euclid had been wrong and it had harbored a whole symphony of accordion players. Any town that admires hardworking burros and dogs is as good a place as any for a man to test his luck, examine his fortunes, maybe even change his fate. Too, there was the high country, and in the near distance that river of pale, silver blue light. So I kept going to South Park and to Fairplay while letting the lovely Dr. Mutzpah's prescriptions reverse my depression's black chemistry. My head emptied of everything save that which had endured and so seemed worthwhile — all those pieces of wild country and layered sunlight and the fast-moving water of high country rivers, wild fish, and the few friends that had somehow stayed with me.

In Fairplay, after weeks of running into each other, Kiwi LaReaux, Swami Bill, and I became close friends. Eventually, I told them how I had managed to show up in Fairplay, how I had fallen from grace, been bounced out of one paradise after another. The morning I told them about my previous life, a life that now seemed so long ago and far away, we were spending a splendid autumn morning off County Road 787 between Alama and Mount Boss, wandering about the haunting trees of the Bristlecone Pine Scenic Area. Kiwi LaReaux believed the trees were bathed in perfect auras, that they glowed like flames of pure burning oxygen. Too, the place was a favorite tourist stop. Easy pickings for Swami Bill, who set up his portable card table in the parking area, piling it high with what he called "socialist magic," great and harmless trinkets, wares cheap enough for anyone to afford — singing crystal bowls, rain sticks, music spheres, cosmic OM tuning forks, and Swami Bill's boxed set of subliminal self-help tapes.

Kiwi LaReaux and I walked among the ancient pines, bent and gnarled and twisted by the unyielding press of weather and time. Kiwi LaReaux told me that bristlecone pines are among the oldest living things on the planet. Up on the high rounded shoulders of the Mosquito Mountains, the ancient trees are drenched for months at a time in a sharp-edged, cold Arctic light.

Kiwi LaReaux told me that the bristlecone pines spoke to her.

"And what do they say?"

"The same thing over and over again," said Kiwi LaReaux.

"And what's that?" I said.

"Time flies," said Kiwi LaReaux.

"Time flies."

From The Bright Country

Coutresy of the Gibbons family

15

ROBERT GIBBONS

They had overprinted *The Patchwork Time*, and the printer wanted a release to melt the plates. During that time I made these dumb remarks about Knopf's wife's commentary. She was prominent in the company. She would get a lot of books from Europe. Finally, he wrote to me and said, 'It's time you heard from the head of the house.' I think that I could have redeemed myself by admitting I had made an ass of myself. But I didn't. It may be that none of these works was publishable as written.

A Promising Start

ROBERT GIBBONS, NEARLY EIGHTY, SAT IN THE well-worn living room of his large home in Lanett and discussed a disastrous career mistake.

By the late 1940s he was regularly publishing short stories in *Esquire*, *McCalls* and other national periodicals. He had published two novels with Alfred A. Knopf and was working with his editor on the third.

"I don't know why it stopped. I had a bust up with Knopf over my third book. I was ill-advised by my literary agent to hold out for an advance rather than give in to corrections Knopf wanted. I have never been able to place any novels with any other publisher since then. That novel was titled *Rebel's Gate*. I got the editor at Knopf to look at all of them after that, but once I had offended Mr. Knopf there was no way I was going to get a book at that press.

"My editor at Knopf was Harold Strauss. He had been Steinbeck's editor. He would have published *The Waters of Espiritu Santo* [Gibbons' fourth novel]. I sent it to Viking and Pascal Covici sent it back and said, 'set it aside for three years and ask yourself why you wrote it this way.'

"Before I had my agent, I had had personal contact with Knopf, and the agent made Knopf mad. Knopf felt the agent had intruded between me and the company. The agent was handling my short stories, and he wouldn't work without a novel. I was fussing with

Harold Strauss and I was ugly. I shouldn't have said the things I did.

"They had overprinted *The Patchwork Time*, and the printer wanted a release to melt the plates. During that time I made these dumb remarks about Knopf's wife's commentary. She was prominent in the company. She would get a lot of books from Europe. Finally, he wrote to me and said, 'It's time you heard from the head of the house.' I think that I could have redeemed myself by admitting I had made an ass of myself. But I didn't. It may be that none of these works was publishable as written.

"Sure they would have worked with me and brought me along. Harold Strauss stopped to see me and wanted to get me back. It took years, maybe ten years. I knew I had made a mistake as soon as I had sent my fifth novel [*Generations*] out. It was eighteen-hundred pages and needed reworking.

"I'm not trying to market my books. After a few disappointments I kind of gave up. I wasn't temperamental, I was just stupid.

"For a number of years I covered the disappointment with alcohol, but I finally had to give that up. Maybe that's one of the reasons I drank so much was I wasn't able to handle the rejection. . . . I haven't [drunk alcohol] in twenty-five years. It goes with writers and it goes with English departments as far as I know. I don't think drinking had any ill effects on my writing. I still wrote *Generations* and *The Waters of Espiritu Santo*."

Mr. Gibbons is a thin man who wears shoulder-length white hair and a beard. His eyes are alert and he walks with the smooth grace of a lazy athlete. He offers humor, humility and some philosophy about his life and career.

"I've written nine novels total. . . . I would say I was six when I started writing because I wrote a story about a pet rabbit which I never owned. It was written on theme paper in Moulton, Alabama. I put it out in the county fair. It won a blue ribbon. I think I thought of writing because my mother was a would-be writer. I had an uncle who cherished visions of being a writer and storytelling was just part of my development.

"I guess I was never anything but a writer and I shouldn't have masqueraded as a teacher. I don't know any other calling that stuck. I would never have gone into teaching if I had continued to make a living as a writer. After *The Patchwork Time* failed commercially and the third book wouldn't sell, I had to pick another profession and I decided on teaching. . . . If I had had to survive only as a writer I don't know where I would have done that. I wasn't a good teacher because I didn't do my scholarship. Teaching allows you to glean enough time to continue writing. . . . Don't we have a theme somewhere about the unhappiness of a great many people? They are unhappy in their work.

"I look for recognition and dream of it in the work that I'm doing now. I hope I'm a better writer now than I was then. It's the seasoning of judgment. Old age, maybe.

"I think both of those books, *Bright Is the Morning* and *The Patchwork Time* have introductory purple passages. I don't think I would do that again. That was fooling around, experimenting without sufficient laboratory experience. . . . Maybe I wasn't able to make my work interesting enough to sell to the book-buying public. By not working at newspapers I missed the opportunity to learn about humanity and the world.

"I'm getting ready to send in a book to the Hackney Awards in Birmingham. It is a novel and it has been rewritten more than once. I think it's a good book. An agent looked at the first version of it, but she didn't think the first version was commercial enough.

"I'm now re-reading this novel and my quota is fifteen pages a day. It is a 330-page novel. Of course, I'll be bitterly disappointed [if nothing comes of it].

"I try to work every day, but I don't have a set time. If I can work early in the morning, that's the best time. I used to be able to stay up and work at night. I can remember working on a novel in Tuscaloosa and working sixteen hours at one sitting.

"I don't spend a great deal of time writing now. I have no routine, no schedule, unless I consider that I'm on some sort of deadline. . . . I never had a routine even when I was writing the first novels. It took years to write a novel . . . I used to write a novel and then discover that I hadn't written it properly. In *The Patchwork Time*, I rewrote it all and put it into that form that you find now.

"There are levels of meaning that help to give substance and texture and help enrich a piece of fiction. Sometimes you put in imagery on purpose. In *The Patchwork Time* that was not a deliberate development. Whatever art is there is there by accident.

"It was some time after I had written *Bright Is the Morning* that I realized I had used my parents' initials in the characters who are the parents of the two boys. It was a long time after I wrote *Bright Is the Morning* before I came to realize how many shadows of autobiography fell over the book."

Then . . .

"*The Waters of Espiritu Santo* is about the fluidity of the universe. All the waters that flow to the sea. If I could get back to it, I could do what Mr. Covici told me to do — look at it and figure out why I wrote it that way and write it another way. I haven't had time. . . .

"I'm probably working on something now that is reflective of that. I'm probably doing what he asked me to do."

∽

More about Robert Gibbons

Profile:

Robert Gibbons was born May 1, 1915, in Tuscaloosa, Ala., to James Booth Gibbons and Anne Walshe Gibbons.

Mr. Gibbons and his nine brothers and sisters lived in twelve Alabama towns. He was educated in the public schools of Vernon, Jasper, Sulligent, Decatur, Moulton and Ashford. Mr. Gibbons earned a B.S. degree from Auburn University and an M.A. degree from the University of Alabama. His first novel, *Bright Is the Morn-*

ing, was published in 1943. In December of that year he left his position as an English teacher at the University of Alabama to serve in the U.S. Navy. After the war, Mr. Gibbons farmed, dug ditches and worked as an agricultural conservation assistant in Brewton and Montgomery before accepting a teaching position at Tulane University. He earned his Ph.D. there in 1957. In 1948, his second and last novel, *The Patchwork Time*, was published. In 1958 he began teaching at Louisiana State University in New Orleans (now the University of New Orleans), where he worked until he retired in 1979.

Mr. Gibbons has been married four times. He has two children from the first marriage and one from the fourth.

Works:

The Patchwork Time, Alfred A. Knopf, 1948.
Bright is the Morning, Alfred A. Knopf, 1943.

Awards:

Rosenwald Fellowship for Fiction in 1943, Alfred A. Knopf fiction fellowship.

Excerpt:

The street looked quiet in the sunlight, as though little besides time ever touched it. It gave the feeling that yonder, away yonder down the road and up the road, the big world kept moving while Pineboro slept. So that by now the town lagged how many Sunday afternoons behind the moving world? Johnny didn't know. It was every day in the week, and every week in the year. But on Sundays the feeling settled thick like dust on a man's heart.

Mac said: "Up here," and turned into a doorway.

"Yeah, I know. I was thinking."

"Don't. It'll give you worms in your head."

They climbed a gloomy flight of stairs that went up between the power company offices and the Citizens Bank. Mac said: "It's like Knox to inherit the oldest building in town. Suits somehow."

"Yeah."

As they reached the top of the stairs Knox opened a door half-way down a hall and put his head out. "That you fellows?"

"Yeah," Mac said.

Knox laughed in schoolboy excitement. "Come on in."

They went down the hall and into Knox's office. Knox had removed his coat and hung it on an old-fashioned clothestree near two dingy windows that looked out on Main Street. Knox said: "Upstairs still holds the heat. Have off your coats." He helped Johnny with his coat, waved his hand vaguely. "Sit down, Somers. Make yourself comfortable. If you can."

Johnny sat down in an old scarred oaken swivelchair that creaked. He looked about and wondered at the age and shabbiness of the office that (so they told in Pineboro) had sent two Daniels to the state senate and one to the U.S. Senate. Cracked plaster walls, a cracked pane in one window, massive untidy desks, and dirt that was not so unclean as it was gloomy.

Suddenly Knox laughed apologetically. "First time here, eh, Somers? Pretty rusty."

"Uhhh — they say it gets the work done."

Knox glimmered with weakling pride for the stronger men who had gone before . . .

From *The Patchwork Time*

Courtesy of the New York Times

16

Howell Raines

"

Writing is easy and pleasurable for some people and hard for others. It's easy and pleasurable now [for me] and was hard in the past. When I went to Washington in 1981, I had been on the *New York Times* for two years. There was tremendous pressure. I never considered myself a good deadline writer. It was very tense, it had to be done right at deadline. Finally I said, 'All you can do is write as well as you can in the time allotted. All they can do is fucking fire you.' That was very liberating. I became one of the best deadline writers on the paper. That had a literary payout for me. I learned to access a creative zone.

"

Why Not Have It

HOWELL RAINES SAT ON A BENCH UNDER A blooming dogwood tree on the campus of his alma mater, Birmingham-Southern College. Students wandered by in shorts. The shine on his shoes ricocheted sunlight. His shirt was crisp and his suspenders rested naturally on his shoulders. He told a story to explain why he remains editorial page editor of the *New York Times* when he could quit and write books full time.

"I met an elderly British man who had been a soldier in Africa and had decided to stay there as a hunter. I asked why he stayed. He walked to the top of a hill and looked out over a vast plain and he said: 'I looked at all that and said why not have it.' I'm the only person from Ensley High School to be asked to be editorial page editor of the *New York Times*. I look at all that and say, 'Why not have it.'

"At the end of my life will I regret not having done what was presented? Then, I don't know.

"It's important to understand the kind of writer you are. The novel does not occupy the place in our literature now that it did in the twenties and thirties. Other kinds of writing have a larger place.

"It may be that "Grady's Gift" [his Pulitzer Prize-winning story about Gradystein Williams Hutchinson, a black woman who worked as a maid for the Raines family] is a more lasting work than I would have produced in another genre.

"The reason I did not go to graduate school for a Ph.D. was that I realized I would have known nothing about the world. Journalism gave me a ticket to see the world. If I want to write about what it looks like in the Oval Office I can do that. I can do more than tell a story with one character's interior feeling.

"There is a balance you strike between the time you spend writing and the time you spend living."

Mr. Raines had just given a speech at the Writer's Conference at Birmingham-Southern. Mrs. Hutchinson was with him and he was introducing her to autograph seekers and well-wishers. There was much talk of helping Mrs. Hutchinson return to school. People were going to arrange rides for her. A raggedly dressed man presented Mr. Raines with a copy of *My Soul Is Rested* to sign. The man explained he had found the first-edition in a Salvation Army store. Mr. Raines left after that to take Mrs. Hutchinson to her small house near one of the last operating steel mills in Birmingham — the Fairfield Works. Mr. Raines and Mrs. Hutchinson walked in the yard, discussing a problem with her house. Mr. Raines told her he could not give her money at that time because of taxes, but he would see what he could do later.

On the way back to Birmingham-Southern for the interview, Mr. Raines discussed his views on racism and the South and particularly Birmingham's role in the battle for equal rights. He said Birmingham can never be punished enough, explaining that he believes certain people and places record an indelible mark in history for particular acts and Birmingham is one of those places. In other words, Bull Connor and the church bombers did for Birmingham what Hitler did for Germany.

"People say to me that they think enough is enough. Well, that's their opinion, they can think what they think. I don't hold that opinion."

Back under the dogwood tree . . .

"When you start writing for a living at age twenty-one the discipline of the newsroom makes writing easier. . . . I had a literary education and went into newspapers and I wrote as well as I could. A general thing that has happened in American newspapers is that they have had to have an almost revolutionary change in the quality of writing. There has been a great emphasis on literary skill.

"Newspapers opened the door in several ways. Writing is an act of exposure. You want it to be perfect. So, when it's not you are abashed. It's painful. Journalism gave me the ability to be a brutal editor of my literary writing. I threw things out of *Fly Fishing* [*Through the Midlife Crisis*] that I loved. It took me twelve years from the night I typed the first seven pages of *Whiskey Man* until it was published. I rewrote that book a dozen times. I went through striking sentences in the novel and I found the first indispensable sentence on page sixty-five. It's very important for a writer to let go of things."

Mr. Raines took a sip of the soft drink he had bought in the school cafeteria, then looked out toward the campus.

"I wanted to be a writer from my earliest memory. It had to be the influence of growing up with stories told in my ears. Uncle Erskine was a great storyteller. I once took a CBS film crew to interview him and listening to him I realized I was hearing my writing style.

"The moment I realized it was an accessible ambition is when I saw a *Field & Stream* and said to my mother, 'I wish I could write for one of those magazines.' And she said, 'I don't see why you can't.' My mother and that magazine is a specific memory. I wrote in high school secretly and when I got to college I specifically thought I was educating myself to be a writer. I was scared to try. It was intimidating. I knew I had a gift, but every time I would try it, the result would be so bad. You've got to do a lot of very bad writing. Once I got comfortable with doing a lot of bad writing that kind of freed me up.

Another freeing experience came later.

"Writing is easy and pleasurable for some people and hard for others. It's easy and pleasurable now [for me] and was hard in the past. When I went to Washington in 1981, I had been on the *New York Times* for two years. There was tremendous pressure. I never considered myself a good deadline writer. It was very tense, it had to be done right at deadline. Finally I said, 'All you can do is write as well as you can in the time allotted. All they can do is fucking fire you.' That was very liberating. I became one of the best deadline writers on the paper. That had a literary payout for me. I learned to access a creative zone.

"You train the unconscious mind to do what you need to do as a writer. In that instance you are training it to write easily on command as you are ready to write. I load my mind with information and the next day, usually in the shower, I know it's going to start and [the creative time] usually lasts two hours.

"I got writer's block once when the material was too powerful for me. I could not deal with it. After a year I said, 'I'm going to write five hundred words.' I learned this whole technique of doing big pieces in small bites. That's the way I wrote 'Grady's Gift.'

"I have no fear that the writing will leave. It could happen, but I don't fear it. I think I will be writing as long as I am healthy. Worrying about what's going to happen is not going to help you. My belief is that I was put here to write and I'm going to write for a long time. I think I was a slow starter and a slow grower. It's taken me this long to get where I am. . . . I'm just now getting to my time as a writer.

"It's a mystery. You don't know if you can sustain it. It's hard to create art and if you do it, it feels really good and you don't know if you can do it again . . . It's about building a body of work and about publishing a great work if you have it in you. Whatever it takes to make one work like that . . . "

❧

More about Howell Raines

Profile:

Howell Hiram Raines was born Feb. 5, 1943, in Birmingham, Ala. He was reared at 1409 Fifth Avenue West in Birmingham. His father, W. S. Raines, was a contractor and his mother, Bertha Walker Raines, was a housewife.

Mr. Raines graduated from Ensley High School before going on to Birmingham-Southern College where he graduated with a major in English. In 1973 he earned his M.A. at the University of Alabama. Mr. Raines's first job was with the *Birmingham Post-Herald*. He then went to the *Tuscaloosa News*, the *Birmingham News*, the *Atlanta Constitution* and the *St. Petersburg Times*. In 1978 he joined the *New York Times* where he has risen to become editorial page editor. His *New York Times Magazine* story, "Grady's Gift" won the Pulitzer Prize in 1992. His first and only novel, *Whiskey Man* was published in 1977 as was his non-fiction book *My Soul Is Rested*. Mr. Raines's autobiographical *Fly Fishing Through the Midlife Crisis* was published in 1993.

He married Susan Woodley and they had two sons, Ben Hayes Raines and Jeffrey Howell Raines, before divorcing.

Works:

Fly Fishing Through the Midlife Crisis, William Morrow, 1993.
Whiskey Man (a novel), Viking, 1977.
My Soul Is Rested: Movement Days in the Deep South Remembered, Putnam, 1977.

Awards:

Pulitzer Prize, 1992.

Excerpt:

Like many Southerners, I was ruined for church by early exposure to preachers. So when I need to hear the sigh of the Eternal, I find myself drawn to a deep hollow between Fork Mountain and Double Top Mountain on the eastern flank of the Blue Ridge. This is where the Rapidan River plunges through a hemlock forest and through gray boulders that jut from the ferny earth like the aboriginal bones of old Virginia. This is a place of enlightenment for me, the spot where I received the blessing of my middle years. Here, after three decades of catching fish, I began learning *to fish*.

From *Fly Fishing Through the Midlife Crisis*

Joey Ivansco, Atlanta Constitution

17

Paul Hemphill

"

I've found that I'm getting too old to do what I've done on these last two books. All that time on the road is getting harder to do. I like the novel, but I wasn't raised on fiction. I didn't get read to as a kid. I don't have the background for it. There's a whole changing of gears for fiction. You're delivering information, but it's in the abstract. Most good writers of fiction were fucked up in one way or another when they were young and they had to live in a fantasy world. I had a great childhood, white bread and baseball. When I grew up I thought fiction was escapism, not really facing life. The great writers of fiction think it's a greater reality than life.

"

We Didn't Toady

PAUL HEMPHILL: "I COULD HAVE BEEN A LOT more successful citizen, brother, uncle, father if I had not been a writer. Because then I would not have had to delve to this other level. I would have been a lot better if I could have been Uncle Paul, famous newspaper columnist.

"I'll be fifty-nine when I finish the ball player [a non-fiction book about the minor leagues]. I don't think I'll ever be able to get an advance for a novel. I'll have to write the whole damned thing and wait months and months for my agent to go through rejection slips. I could write that one jock novel that I have been gagging at the thought of. I'm going to make myself do it. I'll be left dangling with no security. This has been my way of life for a long time. It becomes a little bit scarier with age.

"The way I look at it is that I rolled the dice. I wrote that first book while I was living off a stipend with the Nieman Fellowship. I was on the "Today Show," [and] everywhere. I thought it was always going to be like that. It never was again. I wound up having part-time teaching jobs and doing freelance magazine work in order to stay alive.

"That's why I'm a freelance writer, because of my old man. He was a freelance truck driver. He owned his own rig. I own my own computer.

"I called my dad and told him I quit the paper and he said, 'Are you out of your mind?' He never could understand that we were on the same path. We were both a bit rash and irrational. We didn't toady."

Mr. Hemphill, bone thin after losing ten pounds during a bout with tuberculosis, smoked non-filtered Camels at a table in Manuel's Tavern near his home in Atlanta. Big-nosed and dog-faced, he evoked the image of a seedy private eye or a sharp-eyed, tired newspaper man.

"It just evolved. It was all an accident. Everybody I knew went to Auburn. An English professor told me I had a way with words and I got into journalism. I became a sportswriter. Then I became a columnist. Then I wrote *The Nashville Sound*. That started selling like crazy and I could get a thousand dollars a month by just calling my editor. It all just kind of grew with no planning.

"The problem with my career is no planning. I look around and see what I want to write about and I write it . . . I had a chance to go to the *Philadelphia Inquirer*, but I was living on St. Simon's Island, going barefoot and living off royalties from *The Nashville Sound*. I can look back and see that if I were thinking about my career it would have behooved me to do that. It would have put me in the vortex of the book publishing industry. It don't count if you're a hot shot columnist in another part of the country. It doesn't really count unless you're living in New York. . . . I don't hang out. I don't like New York. When I wrote my piece for the *New York Times Magazine*, I was just some freelancer from out in the boonies. But [when Howell Raines wrote "Grady's Gift" for the same magazine] they lobbied hard for "Grady's Gift" for the Pulitzer.

"Writers shouldn't be concentrated in New York. I've paid. I'm astonished every time I get another contract. I got a total advance of thirty-five thousand dollars for baseball. My agent's fee is five thousand dollars, there's five thousand dollars for expenses. That leaves twenty-five thousand dollars. That's twelve thousand, five hundred dollars a year for two years. Those [writers who live] in New York, they're getting six figures anyway."

Earlier, seated in his middle-class neighborhood home amid simple antique tables and bookshelves, Mr. Hemphill said: "We pay the bills and we send our kid to [private] school and it's damned expensive. We can't afford to pick up and go to Europe on vacation. My wife left her job with *Atlanta* magazine, and now we have two freelancers in one house. We've got to get insurance and it's tremendously expensive. . . . Mostly people ask me for advice and I tell them, 'Don't do it unless you've got something going or you've married well.'"

At Manuel's he stopped to talk with Manuel Maloof, the owner and former county commissioner. Mr. Hemphill and Mr. Maloof have been friends since Mr. Hemphill's newspaper days in the 1960s.

"I quit newspapers because I'd done it. A daily column six days a week will break your back. They weren't think pieces. I wasn't writing one-liners off the top of my head like Grizzard. I was burned out. I looked around and saw too many guys in their fifties who said, 'One day I'm gonna write my novel.' I don't see how people hold down a job and write a book.

"It took me a while to change from newspapers. Now I love the pace of a book. In newspapers I had stopped growing as a writer. I learned shortcuts. I learned to go out and hang around just long enough. I knew instinctively how much I needed to get one thousand words. I would open the scene, give the message, then pick up the scene to finish it off. I learned how to write it clean on a manual typewriter, and I wasn't growing anymore. I had a million people reading it. I began to feel it was cheap celebrity and I wasn't that good, I felt . . .

"I have no idea how good I am now. It really begins to wear on you when you don't sell. I know that's not what we're supposed to worry about. [But it bothers you when] nobody reads what you have to say."

It can also be bothersome when others do read your work. Hemphill, who has struggled with alcoholism, details many of his personal problems in his memoir, *Leaving Birmingham*. He talks of his father's alcoholism and his animosity toward his sister's husband. He also details his first marriage and painful divorce.

"Beware of writers for they will sell you out. Smart people just stay away . . . If you're going to write something, write it all the way. *Leaving Birmingham* damaged my sister and my brother-in-law. It hurt them and it hurt me, too. My sister wrote a letter that said she was deeply hurt by the book. . . .

"Let me tell you about a writer's nightmare. I was on the "Tim Lennox Show," a live call-in radio show [in Birmingham]. The first hour went great. We were having conversations on the air. He broke at 11 a.m. for the news and he said, 'We've got all these calls.' I said 'Tim, I just can't stay any longer.' As I was driving to another appointment I heard this voice and I said, 'I think I know this voice.' It was my ex-sister-in-law. He let her go on for ten minutes. It was a diatribe about how can I pretend to tell others how to live their lives when I can't live mine. You leave yourself wide open. . . . I'm not going to back off. I'm not going to listen to the good legal advice that Howell got not to write about his [divorce in the book *Fly Fishing Through the Midlife Crisis*]."

Even so, there have been questions about Mr. Hemphill's sincerity. Was he exploiting racism and his ties to Birmingham to sell a book to a New York audience? The book, after all, was rushed through editing so it could be released on the thirtieth anniversary of the bombing of the Sixteenth Street Baptist Church.

"I don't think racism sells in New York. They tend to isolate themselves up there and have their own ideas about what will sell and what won't."

Mr. Hemphill plows ahead. He has written two novels, but he struggles with the medium.

"I've found that I'm getting too old to do what I've done on these last two books. All that time on the road is getting harder to do. I like the novel, but I wasn't raised on fiction. I didn't get read to as a kid. I don't have the background for it. There's a whole changing of gears for fiction. You're delivering information, but it's in the abstract. Most good writers of fiction were fucked up in one way or another when they were young and they had to live in a fantasy world. I had a great childhood, white bread and baseball. When I grew up I thought fiction was escapism, not really facing life. The great writers of fiction think it's a greater reality than life.

"The great American novel has been written: *The Grapes of Wrath*. I wish I could write *Of Mice and Men*. I can't. I wasn't raised on fiction and I can't quite get it.

"One reason to write novels is movies. I've gotten movie money on all of them and they've made a movie out of one. [*Long Gone*, an HBO movie.]

"One of the novels I'm writing is that jock novel. I should have already written it."

∾

More about Paul Hemphill

Profile:

Paul Hemphill was born Feb. 18, 1936, in Birmingham, Ala., to Paul and Velma Rebecca Nelson Hemphill. His father was a truck driver and his mother was a government employee.

Mr. Hemphill was reared in the Woodlawn section of Birmingham. He earned his B.A. in English from Auburn University in 1959. After graduating, he went to work as a sportswriter for the *Birmingham News*. After a brief stint in public relations, he returned to newspapers, working at the *Augusta Chronicle* and the *Tampa Tribune*. He took a job as a columnist with the *Atlanta Journal* in 1964 and he remained there until leaving to write full time in 1969.

He wrote his first book, *The Nashville Sound: Bright Lights and Country Music*, in 1969 while he was a Nieman fellow at Harvard University. While Mr. Hemphill has written two novels, his greatest love is the non-fiction book. His work often has focused on his native South, dealing with subjects such as racism and civil rights. Mr. Hemphill relies on autobiography, writing books about his experience with his family and his native Birmingham. He deals openly with his struggle with alcoholism, a divorce and the travails of mending a torn family.

Mr. Hemphill is married to Susan Farran Percy and they live in Atlanta. They have one child, Martha. He has three children — Lisa, David and Molly — from his first marriage.

Works:

Leaving Birmingham: Notes of a Native Son, Viking, 1993.

King of the Road (a novel), Houghton Mifflin, 1989.

Me and the Boy: Journey of Discovery — Father and Son on the Appalachian Trail, Macmillan, 1986.

The Sixkiller Chronicles (a novel), Macmillan, 1985.

Too Old To Cry, Viking, 1981.

Long Gone (a novel), Viking, 1979.

The Good Old Boys, Simon & Schuster, 1974.

Mayor: Notes on the Sixties, Simon & Schuster, 1971.

The Nashville Sound: Bright Lights and Country Music, Simon & Schuster, 1970.

Awards:

Nieman fellow, 1969; Literary Achievement Award from the Georgia Writer's Association, 1970; Distinguished Achievement by Alumni Award from Auburn University, 1985.

Excerpt:

Needing more room, we moved into a three-bedroom rental frame house that was three blocks away on a hill overlooking East Lake Park. My mother was full of herself by now, having survived the Depression and given birth to one boy and one girl, and she became a serious churchgoer for life, beating a regular path to the cozy little Lake Highlands Methodist Church up the street, Sunday mornings and Wednesday nights and half the day on Saturdays, hell or high water, good times or bad. My father never went if he could find an excuse, but these days he seemed to have something big on his mind, something churning inside, plenty to keep him out of church. He was spending a lot of time out front with his dump truck, parked half in the street and half on the sidewalk, peering under the hood and inspecting the mechanism in the rear end that raised the bed in order to dump a load, then standing back for a long look, like an artist sizing up a landscape before painting it. One day when he brought the truck home it had cylindrical fifty-gallon gas tanks strapped to the sides. Another day he arrived and it wasn't even a dump truck anymore; the dump bed was gone, replaced by a fifth wheel he had salvaged from a junkyard. And the next thing we knew, the former dump truck rolled up towing a flatbed trailer he had bought with three hundred dollars he had borrowed somewhere. On a Sunday morning when we walked back home from church we saw him fiercely sawing two-by-fours and bolting them to the trailer to make sideboards. When a neighbor came by to ask him what the hell all the racket was about, Daddy told him, "There's a lot of stuff gonna need haulin', and I thought I'd help 'em out."

What happened was downright heroic when you weigh all of the circumstances, and it changed our lives forever. In January of '41, with Birmingham's furnaces lighting up the sky all over town on the eve of the war, my father made a deal to haul a load of hatch covers for tanks and ships from a Birmingham foundry to Portland, Oregon, three thousand miles away. He would be pulling the load over the southern Rockies in an untested converted dump truck that had no heater, no radio, no chains, no insurance, certainly no power steering or power brakes. Here was a twenty-nine-year-old whose only experience on the open road had been as a teenager driving a Model A Ford three hundred miles out of the Tennessee hills, and now he was going to strike out across the continent and learn over-the-road trucking in one impossible lesson. All he had when he left one bitterly cold morning was enough cash for gas and oil and occasional snacks, a thermos full of coffee, sandwiches Mama had made and wrapped, a road map, a bill of lading, several army blankets, and a kerosene heater on the floorboard. He would be back, he told us, when he got back. And off he went.

From *Leaving Birmingham*

Place

Courtesy of the University of Cincinnati

18

ANDREW HUDGINS

It's the nature of what you can do. Why is one person a novelist and another a songwriter? I've tried to write stories and I get bored. They seem to go on forever. My wife writes short stories and I can hear her in there just happily typing away for four to six hours. I go to the desk for fifteen to thirty minutes and then stomp around and then write some more. Poetry is so distilled. I like that character. It's the difference between whiskey and beer. I like whiskey. . . . Failed poets become novelists. A lot of people think they can become poets. Poets become poets.

It Takes Faith

THERE IS A TOUGHNESS ABOUT ANDREW Hudgins. A solid Southern toughness with a healthy dose of that hard, country sense of humor.

"When I read these in the South, people laugh along," he said of his autobiographical book of poems *The Glass Hammer*. "In the North, people come up and want to talk about dysfunctional families. . . . [I think] this book came out more comic. The Southern sense of humor is sort of cruel. . . . You can recognize Southern poetry the same way you recognize Southern fiction. Southern poetry tends to be more narrative and concerned with the landscape of the family. It affects even the style. Southern writers seem to be more storytellin'. When people talk about Southern writing they tend to want to pigeon-hole you and regard you as a regional writer."

" . . . I used to find myself defending myself because I was Southern. I used to get into those battles defending things I didn't want to defend. I feel there is less of that going on. [Being Southern] is interesting, but it's in no way the totality of what I am. It annoys me when people pigeon-hole themselves. It seems sort of pitiful."

Mr. Hudgins's build and often his mannerisms evoke Buster Keaton. He seems nervous, bending at the waist to look around a corner as if he half expects a building to fall on him. He moves through the Quincy's in Albertville on this overcast August day like a turkey in the woods, wily and a tad paranoid. Mr. Hudgins gets the joke. He layers conversation with humor, from his Southern phrasing to his interesting viewpoint on life's more unpleasant tasks.

"Houghton Mifflin [publishers of three of Hudgins' books of poetry] is not a charitable enterprise. I've always earned back my advances. They are fifteen hundred dollars. That's small. It's irrelevant what my royalty is. I probably put more money into it than I make. I put five hundred dollars' worth of books in the mail to scholars and reviewers. Also I spent a week and a half of my life writing letters to every reviewer I could think of. [But] I don't have the gonads to go into a bookstore and demand that they stock my book. They treat you like a pervert, like something that's stuck to their shoes.

"I've been pretty lucky. My current editor has never put any pressure on me at all. But it's become clear that publishers are quite aware who's making money for them and who's not.

"I don't have the desire to write something because I know it's going to sell. My wife and I have tried to think up projects that would be honest and would sell, but it's hard to do.

"I'd quit teaching in a heartbeat if I got rich. Well, that's not true. I'd probably cut back and do it occasionally. I'm good at teaching writing, so I like to do it. It's a false question, because it's not going to happen. It behooves me to make my peace with teaching and to find a way to take time off for writing. . . . Making money and quitting teaching becomes something there is no need to think about. I teach writing at a research university and they have to give me time to do my writing. . . . People who complain forget how hard it is to work forty hours [and write]."

Time for Mr. Hudgins is not measured in forty-hour weeks.

"Some poems come fairly quickly, others can drag on for years and years. . . . Sometimes they can come as quickly as two or three months. Mostly these things are long-term things. You have to have a lot of patience.

"You push it through to a version in a week and then come

back to it in a couple of weeks. After a while you have a pile of things built up that are in different stages and you can pull them out and push them along. . . . It takes faith. You work and work and follow your instincts without knowing what you're doing and suddenly you hit this kind of flow. . . . It's that place that after a certain amount of work it just falls into place. You've got to put that ninety percent of hours into it before you get that ten percent where it all falls into place.

"Sometimes I read a poem before going to bed and let it work. It's that kind of intricate going back and forth between the intellect and unconscious. You trust your instincts and examine them [the poems] intellectually later.

"Mostly I write until I find the movement of the poem. Once I've got that figured out I go back and cut out everything that doesn't belong. It's time-consuming. I've used up a lot of paper."

Mr. Hudgins writes with a Papermate pen on legal pads. He writes the entire poem over each day, neatly pressing the pen to the paper. Each poem is completely rewritten by hand each time changes are made.

"There are many paths. I'm just in the habit of writing with a pen because I've never wanted to do anything else."

Mr. Hudgins spends four hours a day three or four times a week writing. Writing time includes "stomping around and reading and going to make a cup of tea." He often talks of his type of "nervous system" and how it leads him to write shorter pieces.

"It's the nature of what you can do. Why is one person a novelist and another a songwriter? I've tried to write stories and I get bored. They seem to go on forever. My wife writes short stories and I can hear her in there just happily typing away for four to six hours. I go to the desk for fifteen to thirty minutes and then stomp around and then write some more. Poetry is so distilled. I like that character. It's the difference between whiskey and beer. I like whiskey. . . . Failed poets become novelists. A lot of people think they can become poets. Poets become poets.

"Getting started is the hardest part. When I'm halfway through I can sit at the desk happily for hours and hours. When I am starting I get high-strung and nervous and jumpy. Each time I go through it it's getting cleaner and I'm happy.

"The hardest thing with students is they don't understand that the more you write, the more it gets finished. That was a hard thing for me to learn. People think it's gushing out your own emotions onto the page. Few people can stick to it and find it's more complicated than that.

"The discipline of poetry is very close, very focused . . . Poets who try to write fiction leave you with a sense of being cramped, there's no elbow room. Fiction writers who try to write poetry leave you with a baggier sense. The poetry tends to be sloppy. Fiction and poetry pacing is different.

"I've been scratching out these things since I was in high school. When I first started, it was garbage. My first published poem was in the *Mississippi Review* when I was a senior in college, but that doesn't count. It wasn't a very good poem. I wrote more when I was younger because I didn't know what I was doing. I tried to write every day when I was a kid. I was trying to learn, putting my time in. It's like any other skill. It's not just a skill, but skill is necessary.

"When I graduated from Huntingdon my department chairman tried to convince me to get an MBA. Nobody told me I was any good. The thing I wanted most in the world was to go to Iowa [to the master of fine arts program], and they turned me down flat. That was pretty devastating. I taught the sixth grade for a year and that was terrible. Then I got in at Alabama and I scrambled to do that academic work for the first time in my life. It was put up or shut up . . . Grammar is important now; learning how sentences are put together. I have a fairly firm sense of the possibilities of a sentence.

"Poetry is the only thing I've always done as hard as I could at my highest level. There's a limit to what you can put yourself wholeheartedly into . . . When the first book came out I was thirty-four. I'd worked steadily and that was my ultimate goal. You get crazy after a while and think it's never going to happen. When I first got that book in hardcover I just sat there and looked at it. I would put it down and then go back and pick it up and look at it. I kept picking it up."

❧

More about Andrew Hudgins

Profile:

Andrew Leon Hudgins, Jr., was born April 22, 1951, in Killeen, Texas, to Andrew L. and Roberta Rodgers Hudgins.

Mr. Hudgins was reared in Montgomery, where he graduated from Sidney Lanier High School. He earned a B.A. from Huntingdon College in 1974 and an M.A. from the University of Alabama in 1976. He did post-graduate study at Syracuse University and earned his M.F.A. from the University of Iowa in 1983. Hudgins taught at Carver Elementary School in Montgomery from 1973–74. He was adjunct instructor in composition at Auburn University in Montgomery from 1978–81 and was a lecturer in composition at Baylor University in Waco, Texas, during the 1984–85 academic year. He left that job to become associate professor of English at the University of Cincinnati, Cincinnati, Ohio, in 1985.

He is married to Erin McGraw.

Works:

The Glass Hammer: A Southern Childhood, Houghton Mifflin, 1994.

The Never-Ending: New Poems, Houghton Mifflin, 1991.

After the Lost War: A Narrative, Houghton Mifflin, 1988.

Saints and Strangers, Houghton Mifflin, 1985.

Awards:

Wallace Stegner fellowship, Stanford University, 1983–84; Yaddo Writer's Colony fellow, 1983, 1985, 1987, 1988; Academy of American Poets Award, 1984; John Atherton fellow at Bread Loaf Writers' Conference, 1985; Society of Midland Authors award, 1986; Texas Institute of Letters award, 1986; Great Lakes Colleges Association New Writers Award, 1987; Alabama Library Association Award, 1987; MacDowell Colony fellow, 1986; NEA fellowship, 1986; Fine Arts Work Center fellowship , 1986–87; Ingram Merrill Foundation grant, 1987; Witter Bynner Foundation Prize, 1988; Poets' Prize, 1988; Alfred Hodder fellow at Princeton University, 1989-90.

Excerpt:

FIST

My daddy slapped my hand against my cheek.
"Don't hit yourself. Why are you hitting yourself?"
He held my wrists. I cried and wrestled. My hands,
completely out of my control, slapped me.
And then I did it to my brother, whom God,
in his great wisdom, delivered unto me
each time my parents left the house. With glee,
I'd smack his pink face till he begged,
and then a little longer.
                Fourteen or so,
I wondered how I'd take a punch if some
drunk in a bar demeaned me or my woman.
I'd stand before the mirror, cock my fist,
and drive an uppercut into my cheek.
"Not good enough," I said. "You flinched."
I crawled up off the floor and tried again.
                From *The Glass Hammer*

Joan Bingam

19

ALBERT MURRAY

I'm interested in literature. I want to be the American writer. I don't give a shit about being black or white. People refuse to look at human nature for what it is. You hear Jesse Jackson all the time going on about black on black crime. What is abnormal is some guy killing somebody he doesn't know.

A Mobile Boy

ALBERT MURRAY'S RHYTHM COMES AT YOU, reaching, pushing. You wonder if this is in his head or if he's drawing from the ocean, from the wind, from the immeasurable foot poundings of New York City. He says he's just looking out from his spot high in the spyglass tree.

Mr. Murray's fictional character Scooter climbs a chinaberry tree growing next to the porch of his Mobile home in the novels *Train Whistle Guitar* and *The Spyglass Tree*. From that tree, Scooter, a black child growing up in Mobile in the 1920s, sees the world. He sees jazz men dueling on pianos and hopping trains. He sees strength and honor and prejudice. And he sees the rhythm of the wind in the trees. Rhythm and jazz and writing — and Albert Murray.

"[Jazz and writing are] based on resilience and improvisation." Mr. Murray leaned over a small table in a bar in a hotel in Perdido Beach. "In the twentieth century, it's jazz, boy. It encapsulates the American spirit in the twentieth century. It helps you come to terms with the chaos of the twentieth century. It's grace under pressure. The moment of great pressure, the moment of truth, the moment when you write your message. This is when you play your solo. I think my prose should be able to do that."

Discussing *Train Whistle Guitar*, he continues: "'My name is Jack the Rabbit' means I am resilient. You have to climb the chinaberry tree and see the world is big."

Mr. Murray has lived in Harlem for the last thirty years, but he considers himself a "Mobile boy."

"Each novel's got a lot of Mobile in it. I call it the benchmark. It keeps looping back. It's got expansions. What I developed in Mobile and at school is a cosmopolitan attitude toward myself. It's as if the mythology at Mobile College Training School is that some were designated to go out into the world at large.

"It's a point of view. I like the idea of people who do things in a region where they grew up. In my work I never left that base. I call my fiction a point of departure. I'm a Mobile boy. I think of that all the time. A lot of negroes go away and act like they are refugees. I never had that feeling. I consider myself Southern.

"Most black Southerners don't know shit about the Civil War. They go around talking about Africa. They ought to be horse whipped. I'm that kind of Southerner, the kind that can talk about the Civil War like that. It's this business of Southern sensibility. The artist and intellectual with the Southern base. The sound of a locomotive is the basis to black Southern sensibilities. At church it's 'Get on board'; with slavery it was the Underground Railroad. We took the idea of the locomotive and created art."

Mr. Murray writes and creates from what could be considered an unusual perspective — that of a black man raised in the Deep South in the 1920s.

"I never felt racial inferiority, that never occurred to me. You had some whites who were hostile, in the back woods. But on Government Street in Mobile there were restaurants that were not segregated. . . . It was a very complex situation. If they were farmers there really wasn't any segregation because people all helped each other.

"Robert Penn Warren and I talked about how all the relationships that exist between human beings existed in that institution [slavery] also. You had sex, love, hate. [Racial relations] are really much more complicated than the civil rights rhetoric of people with social sciences degrees."

He said the idea that whites owe a debt to blacks is "civil rights rhetoric. Guys are jealous of guys who achieve."

Mr. Murray had addressed the issue the previous night in a speech to the Alabama Council of the Arts: "After all, who [referring to arts organizations] could possibly be more disturbed by the threat that the pressure to be politically correct represents to the ambitions of serious artists who accept the challenge that the great world classics embody?

"Nor, by the way, does it help matters in the least that the pressure and restrictions of political correctness are being exerted in the guise of well-intentioned permissiveness in interest of what our current crop of do-gooders call the empowerment of the downtrodden. Why should anybody's efforts to equate inaccuracy and mediocrity with excellence be indulged?"

At the table inside the hotel: "The Declaration of Independence and the concept of man and the birthright of a citizen did not exist anywhere before [the United States]. Slaves were Americans, non-voting, but they had these sensibilities. There was no freedom in Africa. The chief owned you. They only now got to that crap, the idea that being free means being African.

"I'm interested in literature. I want to be the American writer. I don't give a shit about being black or white. People refuse to look at human nature for what it is. You hear Jesse Jackson all the time going on about black on black crime. What is abnormal is some guy killing somebody he doesn't know."

Mr. Murray said segregationists lost their base of support because "people aren't willing to put their butt on the line to keep [someone] from voting. Nobody's going to jail to keep someone from voting.

"Athletics is reflecting the attitude of the nation. You've got a basic emotional change. Guys who used to bait negroes, they're betting on negroes now."

Later in the day, his small eyes darting to the ocean and then around the room to hotel guests, Mr. Murray said: "The focus of the book is informed by a certain type of insight. A metaphor for this is better than the concept of it. You control it and you know which direction it goes.

"The language catches the reader, but you're controlling it. There are certain challenges that exist for you in literature: One: Can you open up a scene and have it breathless? Two: Can [your character] operate in a higher tempo?"

He recalls a scene from *Train Whistle Guitar* in which Scooter and Scooter's childhood friend attempt to imitate the walk of blues man Luzana Cholly: "You're running through one level where they're just playing as kids. But the kid knows you've got to make sacrifices. That's why the kids have the Luzana Cholly limp, as if they already know something.

"Humor and satire can help people come to terms with actuality."

More advice: "Write about what you know about because then you can get it right. I don't feel pressure when I'm writing. You go back into yourself and say, 'What do I really think about this?' I'm interested in telling how it is to be a human being.

"You run against the clock. You know all that good writing is out there, so you don't compete with them. You try to do the best you can.

"You create the world and the characters in the world and you are a character. So you possess the world. The criticism or feedback is there to let you know you're not hallucinating.

"It's a mistake to place too much emphasis on autobiographical documentation. It's autobiographical, but not documentation. As a writer, you put [characters] in situations."

Then: "Scooter didn't know who he was. There's something liberating about that."

There also is something liberating about writing fiction, Mr. Murray said. "You can possess circumstances and use them as you want."

Yet he waited until he was much older, nearly sixty, before he published his first work of fiction.

"I wrote fiction just when I came to it."

❦

More about Albert Murray

Profile:

Albert Murray was born in Nokomis, Ala., on May 12, 1916, to Hugh and Mattie Murray. He spent his early years in Mobile.

He received his B.S. in 1939 from Tuskegee Institute. Mr. Murray returned to teach composition and literature and to direct theater from 1940 to 1943. In 1943 he joined the Air Force, from which he retired as a major in 1962. He received his M.A. from New York University in 1948. Mr. Murray has studied at several universities, including the University of Michigan and the University of Chicago. He was O'Connor Professor of Literature at Colgate University in 1970 and 1973, Paul Anthony Brick lecturer at the University of Missouri in 1972, writer-in-residence at Emory University in 1978 and Woodrow Wilson Fellow at Drew University in 1983.

Mr. Murray is married to Mozelle Menefee and they have one daughter, Michelle.

Works:

The Spyglass Tree (a novel), Pantheon Books, 1991.

Good Morning Blues: The Autobiography of Count Basie (with Count Basie), Random House, 1985.

Stomping the Blues, McGraw, 1976.

Train Whistle Guitar (a novel), McGraw, 1974.

The Hero and the Blues, University of Missouri Press, 1973.

South to a Very Old Place, McGraw, 1972.

The Omni-Americans: New Perspectives on Black Experience and American Culture, Outerbriedge & Dientsfrey, 1970. Also published as *The Omni-Americans: Some Alternatives to the Folklore of White*

Supremacy, Vintage Books, 1983.

Awards:

Lillian Smith Award for fiction, 1974, for *Train Whistle Guitar*; Litt.D., Colgate University, 1975; ASCAP Deems Taylor Award for music criticism, 1976, for *Stomping the Blues*

Excerpt:

Sometimes a thin gray, ghost-whispering, mid-winter drizzle would begin while you were still at school, and not only would it settle in for the rest of the mist-blurred, bungalow-huddled afternoon, but it would still be falling after dark as if it would continue throughout the night; and even as you realized that such was the easiest of all times to get your homework (even if it was arithmetic) done (no matter what kind of schoolboy you were) you also knew as who hasn't always known that it was also and also the very best of all good times to be where grown folks were talking again, especially when there were the kind of people visiting who always came because there was somebody there from out of town and you could stay up listening beyond your usual time to be in bed.

Their cane bottom chairs and hide bottom chairs and rocking chairs plus stools always formed the same old family-cozy semicircle before the huge open hearth, and from your place in the chimney corner you could see the play of the firelight against their faces and also watch their tale-time shadows moving against the newspaper wallpaper walls and the ceiling. Not even the best of all barbershops were ever to surpass such nights at home.

From *Train Whistle Guitar*

Life

Mark Gooch

20

EUGENE WALTER

I made a lot of money because of all that film work with Federico Fellini. What I did with all that money was I gave parties. I wouldn't change a thing. Writers shouldn't plan. That's what's wrong with America. You can't plan a life, you can't plan a career. . . . I have money problems now, but I'm managing to pull through. Little by little, I'm solvent. The six cats aren't starving.

"

Youthful Enthusiasm

EUGENE WALTER: "SHOW ME WRITING THAT'S not creative and I'll show you a want ad. . . . I'm a baroque Roman Catholic, Jewish, Druid. . . . When I was in high school I simply told them I didn't take mathematics because Miss Foot was mean and I didn't like mean ladies. . . . When I was a little boy coming out of the library a gypsy woman saw me and said, 'What are you doing with a double aura?'"

It is impossible to interview Eugene Walter. One can only watch him perform. He asks for your address and before the street number he wants to know your astrological sign.

Expatriate, novelist, artist, songwriter, actor, translator, gourmet cook, Mr. Walter spends his days in a small house in Mobile that is more like the littered landscape of a mind than a dwelling. Everywhere are paintings — still lifes and portraits, dark and bright, surreal and real — that seem to run together like wax in the hot Mobile sun.

"Nobody knows what I do and what I've done. I had an operatic debut in Rome in an opera that was written for me.

"I made a lot of money because of all that film work with Federico Fellini. What I did with all that money was I gave parties. I wouldn't change a thing. Writers shouldn't plan. That's what's wrong with America. You can't plan a life, you can't plan a career.

"I have money problems now, but I'm managing to pull through. Little by little, I'm solvent. The six cats aren't starving.

"Americans all decided they wanted security. But those earlier people didn't do that. They would pack all seventeen kids into the wagon and move and cut out woods and make a home.

"I was an only child and was raised by my grandparents mostly. My mother was liberated and she worked. I early learned that if I was quiet I could stay up forever. So I would paint and write and write and paint. My grandparents were very much for letting children be free.

"I'm writing with youthful enthusiasm exactly as I wrote then [as a young man]. I'm still skipping one foot off the ground. Why change now? . . . So many writers are so intense. I prefer to pretend that I toss it off. I have spent two years deciding on a word. *Lizard Fever* [published in 1994 by Livingston Press] sat two years as I waited on the right word for the first line of the first sonnet.

"I work hard, but I don't want anybody to know it. I'd rather have them think I'm just thumbing my nose at them and getting things published. . . . My whole life is writing. More and more I don't go to parties. I prefer to do revisions. I want to get books out. Not articles, books.

"Soon I'll be eighty and I thought, 'My God, I'd better get this work out to publishers.'

"I write quite a bit of fiction. I have a novel, but I'm not happy about it. It's called *Adam's House Cat*. I wrote it over the last five years. Seymour Lawrence wanted it at Little-Brown. He was ready to send me the advance check. I wanted to sit on it. He died, poor darling, of a heart attack.

"I write every day at 5 a.m. I do one hour of translation before I have my coffee. I like to do it while the crazy part of my brain is still there. After that, I work until 11 a.m., then I have a glass of port. I work in my herb garden until about 3:30 and then I take my nap. I sleep soundly until 5 p.m. and then I get up and have a whole new day.

"I used to stay up late, but little by little I started getting up earlier. It's not difficult for me because my brain wakes up with a bang. . . . Then sometimes I'm just lazy. Sometimes in the winter I sleep late. I always watch the cats. If they wake up and open one eye and say, 'What are you doing, you silly boy?' then I go back to sleep."

During a 1992 interview, Mr. Walter's cats prowled the dining room table, dropping their tails into the butter and looking for food. When he finished a piece of chicken, he threw the bones over his shoulder into the kitchen for the cats. Rubbing a cat's back, he talked of his career.

"It's the Sagittarian thing. [We] are always happy when we've got several things to contemplate. I'm a triple Sagittarius. We have to have six pots on the stove or we bring none to boil. . . . Over the years I've gotten a whole repertory of verses and it's time to publish them. I've published two and I have three in manuscript.

"It's harder for genuine writers to be published. Publishing houses all belong to corporations now. Now they say the 'publishing industry.' Once upon a time, every little town in the Deep South had a printer-publisher. They all had little books. It's bad that it's in New York. A lot of those people wouldn't know a sonnet from insecticide. I don't want to hear anything New York publishers have to say. The more original you are, the harder it is to get published.

"You should look toward independent publishers if you are a writer. They do books Alfred Knopf would have been proud of. They have good binding and good jackets, unlike Doubleday books where the pages fly across the room after the third reading."

Mr. Walter's life comes stream-of-conscious on his fluty voice. His soft tones rise and fall over terms of endearment — "honey," "darling," "dear" — like a brook over smooth stones.

"Fellini wanted me to appear in *Eight and a Half*. I wanted to do an interview with him for the *Transatlantic Review*. But he would say to me to translate a script for him or work with him on this or that. This went on for years.

"Finally I made up an interview. And then later, when he was interviewed by the *New York Times* he quoted extensively from the interview I made up. He said, 'Thanks for the interview.'"

Mr. Walter said he translated five hundred movie scripts during his twenty-five years in Rome and hosted a number of memorable parties for the likes of Isak Dinesen, Judy Garland, Muriel Spark and John Cheever.

"John Cheever lived at the Palacio Doria, a few steps from me. He had a kind of nastiness. He had a hangover all the time. His wife had a quiet smile the whole time he was carrying on. I told them I was going to outlive them all and write memoirs."

In a room with a grandfather clock in which are enshrined a "unicorn horn" and "one of Tallulah Bankhead's pubic hairs," Mr. Walter talked about the old gypsy who told him of his double aura when he was a child.

"She told me, 'You will never be rich, but everything you want will naturally come to you.'"

❧

More about Eugene Walter

Profile:

Eugene Walter was born Nov. 30, 1927, in Mobile, Ala., to Eugene and Muriel Sabina Walter.

He attended Spring Hill College, the University of Alabama's Mobile Extension Division, the Museum of Modern Art in New York City, the New School for Social Research at New York University, the Alliance Francaise, the Institute *Brittanique de la Sorbonne* and the Institute Dante Alighieri. Mr. Walter served as associate editor of *Botteghe Oscure* from 1950 to 1959, of *The Paris Review* from 1951 to 1960, of *Folder* from 1951 to 1954, of *Whetstone* from 1953 to 1958, of *Intro Bulletin* during 1957-58, and of the *Transatlantic Review* after 1959. He was a prize-winning scenic designer for more than sixty stage productions in the New York area. Mr. Walter was an actor who played character parts in films, chiefly Italian. He also was a musician who played recorder with the Ancient Instruments Society in Alabama and was a founder and first manager of the Mobile Symphony Orchestra.

Mr. Walter was a U.S. Army Airways Communications System cryptographer from 1942 to 1946.

Mr. Walter lives in Mobile, where he continues to publish poetry and work on a novel.

Works:

Lizard Fever, Livingston University Press, 1994.

Hints & Pinches: A Concise Compendium of Herbs, Spices, and Aromatics with Illustrative Recipes and Asides on Relishes, Chutneys and Other Such Concerns, the Longstreet Press, 1991.

The Likes of Which, Decatur House Press, 1980.

American Cooking: Southern Style, Time-Life Books, 1971.

Love You Good, See You Later, Charles Scribner, 1964.

Singerie-Songorie, Willoughby Institute (Rome), 1958.

Monkey Poems, Noonday, 1954.

The Untidy Pilgrim, Lippincott, 1954.

Mobile Mardis Gras Annual, Haunted Book Shop, 1948.

Jennie the Watercress Girl, Willoughby Institute [Rome), 1947.

Awards:

The Lippincott Fiction prize in 1954 for *The Untidy Pilgrim*, the Sewanee-Rockefeller Fellowship in 1956 for *Monkey Poems*, the O. Henry Citation in 1959 for the short story, "I Love You Batty Sisters."

Excerpt:

Down in Mobile they're all crazy, because the Gulf Coast is the kingdom of monkeys, the land of clowns, ghosts and musicians, and Mobile is sweet lunacy's county seat. I can tell you that's the truth. I know. You used to say you were never the same after living there, and I reckon I'm not either. Few years there done fixed me up. Which is what I want to tell you about. People have been saying of me, "Hasn't he changed?" and "My, he is certainly different," and the thing is, they're right, I *have* changed, but it's not some change you can point at with your finger and say lookathere, see-what-I-mean. It's more subtle than that, and it occurred in strange degrees and lapses, quick and slow, long and short, noted and unheeded. I suppose it might be considered a change from country boy to somewhat citified boy, if you honestly believe in those distinctions. I don't, myself, especially after a glimpse of New York. Some people would say I've become civilized, others would say I've gone to hell with myself. What is civilized, I ask you, and as far as that goes, what is going to hell?

From *The Untidy Pilgrim*

ABOUT THE AUTHOR

Bill Caton is a native of Alabama, reared in Birmingham. He graduated from Auburn University in 1980 with a bachelor's degree in journalism and has worked as an editor and writer for newspapers and magazines. His children's book, *Josh and the Flat Cows*, was published in 1994. He lives in Birmingham with his wife, Ann, and their son, Joshua.